WEDDINGS
from the HEART

BOOKS BY DAPHNE ROSE KINGMA

365 Days of Love

The Book of Love

Finding True Love

True Love

A Lifetime of Love

To Have and To Hold

Heart & Soul

The Future of Love

The 9 Types of Lovers

The Men We Never Knew

Coming Apart

WEDDINGS
from the HEART

Contemporary and Traditional Ceremonies
for an Unforgettable Wedding

DAPHNE ROSE KINGMA

Conari Press

Red Wheel/Weiser, LLC
With offices at:
500 Third Street, Suite 230
San Francisco, CA 94107
www.redwheelweiser.com

ISBN: 978-1-57324-861-7

Library of Congress Cataloging-in-Publication Data

Kingma, Daphne Rose.
   Weddings from the heart : contemporary and traditional ceremonies for an unforgettable wedding / Daphne Rose Kingma. —2nd ed.
          p.   cm.
   ISBN: 0-943233-94-1 (trade paper)
   1. Marriage service—United States.   I. Title.
HQ745.K48   1994
392'.5—dc20   94-30922

Cover Photography: © Corbis Images/PictureQuest
Cover and Book Design: Maxine Ressler

Printed in Canada
TCP
10 9 8 7 6 5 4

ESPECIALLY
FOR YOU

*Because You Want to Have
an Unforgettable Wedding*

your UNFORGETTABLE WEDDING

THIS BOOK IS A COMPENDIUM OF WEDDINGS from the heart. It is designed especially for you if you desire above all to have a wedding that touches your heart and changes your life, a wedding you'll feel the profoundest sense of joy in recalling, long after the confetti and rose petals have been swept from the driveway.

A wedding from the heart is a ceremony that springs from your own deep feelings and arouses such feelings in all those who witness it. It is a sacred chalice for your love, an elegant frame for the portrait of you and your beloved as you are united by high hopes, profound emotion, and a desire to honor your relationship by expressing it as a commitment made in the presence of family and friends.

Not necessarily traditional, but more than a mere formality, a wedding from the heart is a truly emotional experience, one borne up on a flood of feeling rather than homogenized through the heavy-handed application of familiar conventions. It has as its hallmark the beliefs that your relationship is a treasure and that your wedding day will be one of the most precious in your life. In creating a wedding from the heart, you recognize not only that your wedding is a symbol of your love, but also that it can be a deeply moving experience for everyone involved, even for you as you plan and organize it.

3

More than a major social event, a heartful wedding is more about what you say, do, and feel than what you wear or how many courses you serve at the reception dinner. It's about love and not about impressing people; it's about *your* love—what it means to you, where you want it to take you, and what hopes you have for it.

This isn't to say that your beautiful dress and the exquisite flowers aren't important, nor that you shouldn't have the traditional photo of you and your new spouse feeding each other a piece of wedding cake. What it does mean is that you will include these things only because they have meaning for you, because they genuinely reflect what you both feel, because they speak to your heart.

A ceremony is a special event that contains formal or ritualized components and which has as the purpose the setting apart and elevating of a particular person or event in our consciousness. We have ceremonies to acknowledge personal achievement, to celebrate national victories and heroes, even to mark our sorrows and losses; but of all our traditional ceremonies, the wedding is the sweetest, because it is a celebration of love. It celebrates possibilities; its attitude is joy; its mood is hope.

But, unfortunately, for all too many of us the beautiful possibilities of the marriage ceremony become gradually eclipsed by the demands of organizing the wedding itself. The endless phone calls, decisions, arrangements, and expenses involved in planning such an event can leave a bride and groom feeling like the frazzled producers of an off-Broadway musical about love and romance instead of participants in a sacred ceremony that celebrates the power of love and the meaning of their particular relationship.

Indeed, weddings can get so bogged down in the endless exigencies of organizing and planning that the experience itself, when it finally occurs, can seem as though it has very little to do with the love that inspired it in the first place. You can get so involved with the rehearsal dinner, the wedding bouquet, and the band at the reception that you forget that the most important part of the wedding is the ceremony itself—the words that are spoken, the promises you make to one another, the bond you create as you enter into marriage.

Everyone wants their wedding to be beautiful, and of course you also want your wedding to flow smoothly—and it will. But all this requires a great deal of effort. Don't lose the spirit of the day by getting so overwhelmed with endless details that you allow yourself to get disconnected from what your wedding is really about—the love you have for the person you're going to marry and the life you want to share in the future.

Keeping these deeper things in mind at every step of the process is what will make your wedding unforgettable, an occasion which, when you call it to mind in the future, or relive it through the photographs or videos, will remind you of the moving, exuberant, tender, passionate, and life-changing feelings that caused you to fall in love in the first place. For long after the champagne bottles have been taken away and you've polished off the last piece of frozen anniversary cake, it is the essence of your ceremony—the words that were spoken, the atmosphere you created through them, and the love and joy you generated through all its special moments—that will take root in your hearts and form the foundation of a love so strong that it can span your life.

Chains do not hold a marriage together. It is threads, hundreds of tiny threads which sew people together through the years.
—*Simone Signoret*

If you want your wedding to be unforgettable, you will want to fashion it in such a way that it truly reflects the uniqueness of your relationship. Because a wedding, whatever its form, symbolizes and celebrates an emotional and spiritual bond, you will want yours to reflect the love that has affected you so deeply that you have decided to change the whole color and texture of your life by getting married. For just as you love the person you're about to marry because he or she is in some way different from all others in your eyes, so you will want to make your wedding unforgettable by creating a ceremony that is as special as the two of you, one tailored to express not only the quality of your love, but also your wonderful quirks, your touchingly special attributes as individuals, and the feelings, wishes, and intentions that you share as a couple.

Thus, although the classic image of a traditional wedding—the bride in white and the groom in a tuxedo saying vows of "'til death do us part"—may be indelibly imprinted on your mind, it may neither fit your particular circumstances nor embrace the range of feelings you want to evoke as the memento of your love. You may want a wedding that resonates with tradition yet includes opportunities for departures from custom, a wedding that truly expresses your own uniqueness.

❧ BUILDING ON TRADITION ❧

Traditional weddings are generally based on the values of society and the church. In addition to honoring the bond between the bride and groom, they invite the new couple to surrender their union to the care and approbation of the larger community. In such ceremonies, marriage can be construed to be somehow at the service of society or the church. The bride and groom are saying, in effect, "through this ceremony we submit our relationship to a larger, more commonly held notion of what marriage is; we will live by society's or the church's definition of what's right."

Because you have purchased this book, you obviously want something other than the strictly traditional ceremony available through your church or synagogue. By providing you with a selection of elements both traditional and contemporary, this book is a gift to that purpose. It invites you to consciously create the wedding ceremony that will have the profoundest meaning for you. For in deciding to create a wedding from the heart, you're saying that you are interested in a more personalized definition of marriage, one that includes a very specific reflection of your love and of what your relationship means to you. You know that love is a feeling—it's what's brought you here; but you also know that marriage is an undertaking that will ask you to mature your love in a way that serves, delights, and challenges you; and it's this that you are wanting to express in your departure from tradition.

Weddings from the Heart encourages you to expand the definition of marriage by reshaping traditional elements in such a way that you can acknowledge time-honored values while creating a highly personalized wedding ceremony. By studying the various components of the ceremony, choosing those that suit you exactly and working together so that what you include reflects what both of you feel, you can create a truly beautiful wedding. Your wedding will be a personalized expression of your values and experiences, as well as of the hopes, dreams, and intentions that are so precious to both of you. Above all, it can become the blueprint for the life you intend to live when you are married.

❧ USING THIS BOOK ❧

The book opens with an essay, *Reflections on Marriage*, which is just that—a discussion of the meaning and attributes of marriage, its emotional and spiritual dimensions. Although this is meant to be a reflective meditation on the undertaking of marriage, a way for you to prepare yourself for creating your ceremony, a great many people have found it such an inspirational statement about the meaning of marriage that they have chosen to use it, virtually unmodified, as the "address" in their wedding ceremony. I have included the essay so that whether you're using it as inspiration for planning your wedding or as part of the wedding itself, its message it will open your heart to the deeper meanings of your marriage ceremony. The book then discusses the meaning of the various parts of the wedding ceremony so you can begin to determine which ones you wish to include.

It next offers five complete contemporary ceremonies, which reflect most accurately, I believe, what a wedding and marriage itself mean in the emotional and spiritual environment we are living in at the close of this twentieth century. They can be used by any couple who choose to honor their union by getting married, no matter what their sexual or lifestyle preference may be. Although none of the ceremonies has been written specifically for the gay or lesbian couple, all have been used, with slight variations, in gay and lesbian weddings. It is relationship itself that we are celebrating here, not the specific configuration of it. The focus is on the power of love to bind us together; to transcend the differences that all too often divide us, and I have chosen, therefore, not to "ghettoize" gay and lesbian relationships by creating a categorically different ceremony for them.

Although each ceremony stands complete in itself, as you study them all you may find that you'd like to use a single one in its entirety or combine selections from several. To assist you in the process, I also have included a civil ceremony, as well as an array of vows, benedictions, and readings from a wide variety of traditions. Those that bear no specific attribution have been written by me. These, too, you can use as is, or modify to accommodate your taste and circumstances. For example, you may want to use the traditional Methodist convocation, then move to selections from this book for the readings, consecration, address, vows, and exchanging of the rings, then perhaps conclude with the traditional benediction of your church. Or, you may want to begin with one of the convocations offered here, have your officiant give his or her own address, use the traditional broken glass of the Jewish faith, and conclude with the Catholic benediction. (In this regard you will note that I have chosen not to include either an entire Roman Catholic or Jewish ceremony, since these are readily available from your parish or synagogue, and they are always performed by a priest or rabbi, with very little room for variation.)

These selections are followed by Ceremonial Flourishes, personal touches that others have added to their weddings and that you may wish to include or adapt to add a special touch to your own.

And, finally, the book contains worksheets to help you formulate your ceremony. This is where you can work out the exact selections for the various parts of your ceremony by following the general format laid out in the worksheets, and inserting such portions as you select in the appropriate place.

Don't be afraid to be adventurous. One kind of mood will be created by relying on tradition, another by using something brand-new; the combination will be unique, inspiring. Certain feelings will be invoked by delving into family and religious traditions, but you are also making something new here—your own wedding. In so doing, you are creating a synthesis of all the traditions you hold dear, as well as an embodiment of the hopes and aspirations which, through your marriage, you hope to bring to fulfillment.

By hand-tailoring your wedding, you can create an occasion that will give you the greatest sense of joy in recalling. In choosing all the elements with care, and in saying words that come from your heart, you will touch the hearts of all those who share this precious day with you and make yours a truly unforgettable wedding.

REFLECTIONS *on* MARRIAGE

MARRIAGE IS THE JOINING OF TWO LIVES, the mystical, physical, and emotional union of two human beings who have separate families and histories, separate tragedies and destinies. It is the merging and intermeshing not only of two bodies and two personalities, but also of two life stories. Two individuals, each of whom has a unique and life-shaping past, willingly choose to set aside the solitary exploration of themselves to discover who they are in the presence of one another.

In marriage we marry a mystery, an other, a counterpart. In a sense the person we marry is a stranger about whom we have a magnificent hunch. The person we choose to marry is someone we love, but his depths, her intimate intricacies, we will come to know only in the long unraveling of time. We know enough about our beloved to know that we love him, to imagine that, as time goes on, we will come to enjoy her even more, become even more of ourselves in her presence. To our knowledge we add our willingness to embark on the journey of getting to know him, of coming to see her, ever so wonderfully more.

Swept up by attraction, attention, fantasy, hope, and a certain happy measure of recognition, we agree to come together for the mysterious future, to see where the journey will take us. This companionship on life's journey is the hallmark of marriage, its natural province, its sweetest and most primal gift. To be married means we belong with someone else, that we are no longer always alone, that we no longer must eat and sleep, dream, wake, walk, talk, think, and live alone. Instead there is a parallel presence and spirit in all that we undertake. We are bridled, connected, attended. We move in the midst of the aura, the welcoming soul-filling presence of another human being, no longer facing the troubling, heart-rending hurts of our lives in isolation. In marriage we are delivered from our most ancient aloneness, embraced in the nest of human company, so that the sharp teeth of the truth that we are born and die alone are blunted by the miracle of loving companionship.

Marriage is also the incubator of love, the protected environment in which a love that is personal and touching and real can grow and, as a consequence of that growth, develop in us our highest capabilities as loving human beings. We are each still and always becoming, and when we marry, we promise not only our own becoming but also our willingness to witness and withstand the ongoing becoming of another human being. That is because in marrying we promise to love not only as we feel right now, but also as we intend to feel. In marriage we say not only, "I love you today," but also, "I promise to love you tomorrow, the next day, and always."

In promising always, we promise each other time. We promise to exercise our love, to stretch it large enough to embrace the unforeseen realities of the future. We promise to learn to love beyond the level of our instincts and inclinations, to love in foul weather as well as good, in hard times as well as when we are exhilarated by the pleasures of romance.

We change because of these promises. We shape ourselves according to them; we live in their midst and live differently because of them. We feel protected because of them. We try some things and resist trying others because, having promised, we feel secure. Marriage, the bond, makes us free—to see, to be, to love. Our souls are protected; our hearts have come home.

In simple terms this means that because we are safe in marriage, we can risk; because we have been promised a future, we can take extraordinary chances. Because we know we are loved, we can step beyond our fears; because we have been chosen, we can transcend our insecurities. We can make mistakes, knowing we will not be cast out; take missteps, knowing someone will be there to catch us. And because mistakes and missteps are the stuff of change, of expansion, in marriage we can expand to our fullest capacity; in marriage we can heal.

Because life is movement, the passage of time equals change. Therefore, when we promise time to one another, we are putting ourselves in the midst of an infinity of change. Implicitly this is also a promise to expand. We will not be cardboard men and women. We will be electric human beings with variegated histories and fabulous unknown futures.

For marriage is more than just the sentimental formalizing of a feeling; it is a vote of confidence, indeed of conviction, that the romantic feeling of love will be enlarged to encompass far more than itself, that both persons will be able, in time, and within the sacred circle of marriage, to infinitely expand.

Change compounded is transformation; and therefore one of the ultimate consequences of marriage is transformation. For so long as we live out our lives in the context of another human being, the changes that accrue in us, that are indeed inspired, required, cajoled, and beaten out of us by our interactions with another—all these will result, in time, in a major transformation of our selves. We would become someone quite different without the person we have married, for it is the alchemy of the relationship itself that transforms us. That which we become in the presence of another person—the person we love most deeply, the person we choose to marry and

We drop like pebbles into the ponds of each other's souls, and the orbit of our ripples continues to expand, intersecting with countless others.

—*Joan Borysenko*

spend our whole life with, the person in whose presence and as a result of whose actions and inactions, words and silences causes us to change, ultimately to transform—brings us inescapably into the being of our highest selves. We become who we were meant to be.

It is precisely at the point at which marriage, the institution, and love, the emotion, intersect that there exist some of our greatest emotional and spiritual possibilities. For marriage is love in the round; marriage is loving in every direction. We marry not only to be loved, to be consoled through the miracle of company, to feel secure, to have a place and a person to whom we can come home, to have our own needs met; we marry also to come into the presence of our own capacity to love: to nurture, to heal, to give, and to forgive.

Marriage is the fearless fathoming of our own depths, a coming face-to-face, in the dark mercurial waters of our endless self-involvement, with the jewel-like treasures of our own submerged capacities for compassion. For love received is needs met; but love delivered is compassion, is the human spirit altered, is our own most whole becoming. In loving we are encouraged to the limits of our most exquisite human possibilities.

Thus marriage is an invitation to transcend the human condition. For in stepping beyond the self-focus of wanting to have only our own needs met, in schooling ourselves in the experience of putting another human being and his or her needs in a position of equal value to our own, we touch the web of transcendence, the presence of the divine.

For loving one another is the beginning of compassion, and compassion generalized is participation in the divine—that experience of life and of the world that paradoxically submerges us in all that exists while at the same time elevating us above it. The compassionate, soul-changing loving of a single other human being connects us most profoundly to the All. And it is in the practice of this radiant other-discovering love that true marriage calls forth the best in us, the most we can ever become.

CREATING *your* CEREMONY

THERE ARE ONLY TWO ELEMENTS ESSENTIAL TO a legally binding wedding: the vows or promises you make to one another and the proclamation by the officiant that you are now married. All other elements are optional. Therefore, in planning your wedding and deciding what you want to include, you have tremendous freedom to create a ceremony that is totally expressive of the two of you.

A wedding is the social portal to married life, a turning point, a marker on the path of your own development that denotes the moment at which you cease to be a solitary person pursuing an individual life and begin taking up the joys and responsibilities of sharing your life with another person. So as you plan the wedding that will stand forever in your memory as the emblem of the moment that delivered you to your new life, you may want to contemplate the meanings of marriage itself. In this way you can discover exactly what you would like to include in your ceremony so it will carry the unique and beautiful meanings that you want to express and hold in memory.

Creating a wedding ceremony is a time-consuming undertaking. It requires careful planning, lots of energy, and, above all, an awareness of exactly what you want to reflect in the precious moments of your wedding. In choosing to create your own ceremony, you have indicated from the very start that you are willing to explore the possibilities—and possible pitfalls—of creating a tailor-made, unique masterpiece with the person you love.

For as you plan your wedding together, you'll come face-to-face with what you really mean to each other, what your values are, what your vision of marriage is, what you expect from and are willing to promise each other, both now and in the future. You'll have a chance to look at the depths of your love, to reaffirm all the wonderful feelings that brought you here in the first place. You'll also have an opportunity to encounter your individual preferences and differences and resolve them. The task of planning a wedding is a little like marriage itself—a process of discovery, an opportunity to grown in love.

If you're wise, you'll use this process as an occasion to deepen your relationship, to work through whatever conflicts may arise, to appreciate each other for the various talents you bring to the project, to have a first experience of creating something that is a reflection of your union.

❧ QUESTIONS FOR REFLECTION ❧

To help you design the perfect wedding, you'll want to keep in mind the following considerations:

1. What do you want to say about your relationship in this public forum? What stories about it do you want to tell? What beliefs about a relationship do you want to reveal?

2. Because your wedding ceremony is the public blueprint for what you expect and hope for in your marriage, what do you want to say about the meaning of marriage, both for your own benefit and for that

of the gathered guests? (Here you may want to keep in mind that a wedding is also a teaching ceremony for those who witness it.)

3. What is the style of your ceremony and what is the image you want to project through it? A theatrical performance, an intimate conversation, a religious ritual, a carnival or festival, a gathering of clans, a formal social event?

❧ FINDING AN OFFICIANT ❧

As you begin the decision-making process, you will want to enlist the counsel of the person who will be officiating at your ceremony, first, to make sure that he or she is comfortable with the kind of ceremony you are envisioning, and, second, to find out if he or she has any suggestions for you. It's also important to choose your officiant early, for he or she is an invaluable resource in planning your ceremony and in answering any questions you might have. In choosing this person, you will want to be sure that he or she is not only willing but able to reflect accurately what you want your ceremony to convey.

In the past, the officiant at a wedding was just that—an official of the church or state. His duty—and it was usually a he—was to make sure that a given relationship would fulfill the standards for marriage as delineated by the church and state. More than finding a proper "official," however, you will want to be looking for someone who can be a spokesperson for you, your values, and your relationship. You will want to find someone who can reflect the quality of your love and speak meaningfully to you and your partner.

Your own minister, priest, or rabbi is, of course, the conventional choice, but if you don't have a strong, personal, or long-standing relationship with this person, you may want to look elsewhere. Following are some ideas for how to "connect" with someone who will be able to express the ideas and emotions you want to convey in your wedding ceremony:

Check in your phone book for churches of different denominations which may appeal to you. Such spiritual orientations as those of the Unitarian Church, Unity Church, Humanist Society, Theosophical Society, and Buddhist centers may reflect a view of life more consistent with your own.

Or try asking a dear or long-standing friend. Sometimes a person who knows you well is the best spokesperson for what you want to say. If this person is not a licensed officiant, you may want to encourage him or her to obtain a license for the occasion. (The Universal Life Church, 601 Third Street, Modesto, CA 95351, licenses individuals to perform legal wedding ceremonies). If your friend doesn't want to go through the process of becoming licensed, consider having this special person deliver the "address"; then a judge, justice of the peace, minister, or rabbi can officiate the formal (and legally binding) parts of the ceremony. In this regard you should know that for legal purposes, it is a person licensed to perform marriages who must make the proclamation of marriage and sign your marriage license. All other parts of the ceremony may be conducted by any person of your choice.

Whomever you consider, be sure to think about the following questions:

Does he or she reflect or embody the spirit you want to create at your wedding?

Do you feel comfortable with him or her? Will you be able to express your preferences about content; speak up about matters of concern in the preparation of the ceremony; voice objections you might have or ask for silly, even seemingly trivial things (like certain pet phrases of yours, for example) to be included in the ceremony?

Do you like the sound of his or her voice? Remember that this is the person whose voice will inspire, instruct, challenge, or out-and-out delight you about the undertaking of marriage, and whose lead you will follow in saying your vows.

Do you have a personal relationship with him or her, a connection that allows you to trust that what he or she will say will be

To fall in love is easy, even to remain in it is not difficult; our human loneliness is cause enough. But it is a hard quest worth making to find a comrade through whose steady presence one becomes steadily the person one desires to be.

—*Anna Louise Strong*

appropriate for the two of you? Or, if this is someone whom you do not know, do you trust that this person has "a sense" of you and understands the uniqueness of your relationship?

What is the fee for his or her services? Judges and justices of the peace normally charge a flat fee, whereas clergy members' fees vary widely. Often they're based on your income, the time involved, and the size of the ceremony. Some fees cover everything—the use of the church, candles, organist, janitorial services—while others do not. And fees aren't uniform—ranging from as little as $50 to as much as $400. Other officiants may charge even more, up to or exceeding $1,000, so be sure to find out beforehand.

Seemingly trivial, but also important (aesthetics, after all, are one of the great joys—and great concerns—at any wedding), will you like what he or she chooses to wear to perform your ceremony? Will it be complementary to the ambiance you want to create? Do you trust his or her taste?

Above all, will you value what this person has to say? Will he or she have delightful, meaningful, moving reflections that will elevate the ceremony from ordinary, generic, and formal to personal, beautiful, and unforgettable? Do you trust that his or her words will provide the inspiration, the message you want to guide you graciously from your past and into this exciting new chapter—married life?

❧ CHOOSING YOUR ATTENDANTS ❧

The people who "stand up" with you at your wedding are a representation of you, and because they will play a very important role in your wedding ceremony, they should be chosen with care. Among other things, they are your "high witnesses"; that is, they stand close to you and, by their proximate presence, agree to recognize now and remember always what transpired on the occasion of your marriage.

If you really want a heartfelt wedding, this isn't the time for fulfilling political, business, or social obligations. Instead, choose people who have shared your life with you, individuals who live in your heart and share your dreams for a life of love and happiness. They may or may not be members of your family. They may be good friends, little children, or a very old person. Be truthful. And daring. Don't stoop to obligation or succumb to convention. Allow the people you choose to bring something of value to your wedding. Pick the friend you haven't seen for years but who was there the fourteen times you broke up in college and can finally celebrate with you. Or include the neighbor who befriended you when you had all but given up on finding love. Choose the brother who always believed in your relationship when your parents pooh-poohed it, or the four-year-old nephew who loves you more than anyone else. Whomever you choose, make it someone who loves you, someone you love.

In making your decision, ask yourself: Why am I asking this person to stand up with me at my wedding? What part of my life has he shared? What aspect of my history will she be representing at my wedding? How do I feel about his or her reactions to the words, values, and ideas that are going to be expressed in the ceremony? When I see this person in the future, will it be a positive reminder of what was expressed?

Will I be happy (or irritated) by this person's presence? Will his personality foibles be an asset or a liability? Would I rather have her among the guests than standing beside me? Would I be sad—would my wedding be less than my dream of it—if he or she weren't there?

Remember, if you include attendants, one or more of them may have the duty of handing you the wedding rings, helping you with your dress, or holding your bouquet. Will they behave in the way you'd like them to; that is, will they be relaxed and dignified enough to suit you, vibrant or serious enough to create the mood you're after? Will they be willing to help graciously with mundane matters—cutting the ribbons on your bouquet, straightening your dress, or running out to buy extra hat pins for a marooned boutonniere?

Don't be afraid to do what your heart tells you. A male friend of mine had four women as his attendants, and a woman I know selected her best male friend to be hers. Maybe your beloved is the only person you want to stand beside you. If that's the case, don't be afraid to scrap tradition and stand at the altar together, in your own loving recognizance, with the officiant. In breaking with tradition you create tradition, tradition that moves from what's "proper" and expected to what truly springs from the heart.

✧ CREATING THE COMMUNITY ✧

The "community" of your wedding is your guests—the people you've invited to share in the intimate moments in which you make your love public and state your lifetime intentions to each other.

In the past, the guests at a wedding served a variety of purposes. Sometimes it was to demonstrate the power of two families coming together, others times to display of the status of the bride's or groom's parents—to say nothing of being an opportunity for parents to show off the beauty or achievements of their children. We've all heard the expression that he or she "made a good marriage," meaning that he or she improved his or her financial or social status. And we've heard about "important" weddings, which means that all the "right" people were there.

Such expressions may hold importance in the world of politics, society, and commerce, but a wedding of the heart is a binding of the spirits of all who have gathered to shore up, celebrate, acknowledge, and encourage the two people creating a new life together.

Thus the guests at your wedding are your body of witness. To witness means to pledge, to make material, to bring into form. So when you choose a group of people to share the occasion, you are really asking them to ensure that in the future you will enact what you have publicly avowed through the vehicle of your wedding ceremony.

Viewed in this fashion, the guests at your wedding are not the largest number of people you know, the ones who will bring the best presents, or even all your distant relatives. They're the people who mean the most to you, those who have shared your life, who've provided for and protected you, who have nourished your spirit and sorted out your emotions, who've been there to help you through the hard times. They're the ones who have loved you through thick and thin, who've watched you grow up, celebrated your every transformation, believed in you, encouraged you, and shared the significant aspects of your life.

So to create a true wedding community, invite the people you love, those whose paths have crossed yours and tugged on your heartstrings along the way. In planning your guest list, ask yourself the following questions: Who are the ten people above all whom I'd like to be there, the ones I'd be absolutely heartbroken if they didn't attend? If I could ask everyone I'd like to, who would be on the list?

Now, working from both ends of that spectrum, who are the people between the extremes (taking into account the accommodations, of course) that you'd really want to share in your special day? What is the common thread that ties all these people together? The role they've played in your lives? The love you have for them and they for you? The social or business life you share? How will they "gel"—in spite of their differences and diversity—to become the community that will send you off into the joy of marriage?

Is there anyone you automatically included whom in your heart of hearts you'd rather not invite? An obligatory friend? A political concession to one of your parents? A colleague you really don't like? If there is such a person or persons, feel free to say, "It was a very small and private wedding; I'm sorry, but we couldn't include everyone."

In some instances, for difficult emotional reasons, people prefer not to have their parents at their wedding. If you have some painful unfinished business that you've been unable to resolve, don't spoil your wedding by "inviting them anyway." Instead, respect your need to celebrate and move forward in your life without their participation at this time; and for their sakes, have the courtesy to conduct your wedding in private. Perhaps the blessings of your marriage may also, someday, include a mending of this rift.

❧ SELECTING INVITATIONS ❧

The same considerations that apply to guest lists and attendants hold true with your wedding invitations. You will want your announcement to the world that you're going public with your love to be a reflection of your relationship's uniqueness. There's always the conventional "Mr. and Mrs. So and So request the honor of your presence," but what do *you* really want to say? Do you like the standard black on white formal invitation, or would you prefer to write out your invitations in your own hand? Do you want professional calligraphy? or a cellophane Technicolor collage?

More and more couples feel that since they are not stepping directly out of their parents' homes and into marriage—they're over twenty-one, they've been out in the world for a while, been through a relationship (or even a marriage) or two—they want this reflected in their invitations. Some examples: "Donna and John invite you to witness their wedding and to share in a celebration of marriage"; "Don and Mary Jane invite you to participate in a ceremony to celebrate 'the unfolding of love'"; "Stan and Barbara ask you to stand in the sacred circle of witness as they recite their wedding vows."

On the other hand, perhaps your families have been so supportive that you want to mention *both* sets of parents in your invitation: "Mr. and Mrs. X and Mr. and Mrs. Y invite you to celebrate the marriage of their children . . ."

Once again, my suggestion is that you follow your heart and express what is true for you, rather than routinely following the customary form. This goes for the design of the invitation as well. There's more than white vellum for a wedding invitation; be creative. One couple I know sent theirs in paper-covered mailing tubes, another in seed packets. Still others have used beautiful handmade papers, a photograph of themselves, or replicas of antique Valentines. Let yourself go! The ambiance you create with the invitation will carry over to the ceremony itself.

❧ CHOOSING THE SETTING ❧

The location of your wedding is every bit as important as the words you say, the people who stand up for you, and those you invite to witness the ceremony. Wherever you choose, make sure it holds special meaning for you, that it's a place you'll want to remember and return to—if not literally, at least in memory—and not just one that's convenient or available. Place creates mood, and mood creates the quality of memory.

Do you want a formal church setting? the ballroom of an elegant hotel? a beautiful outdoor park? a meadow at the edge of a cliff overlooking the sea? Do you want have it someplace special to you, such as the old inn where you spent your first romantic weekend, your parents' garden, or a holiday spa you'll love to return to?

Also consider whether you want to hold the ceremony and reception at the same location. Combining them in one place certainly has benefits—it minimizes traffic and parking problems and saves time (and often money too)—but perhaps at the price of convenience. A couple I know had their hearts set on marrying in a pine grove, but they couldn't work out the logistics of serving food in the middle of the woods. So they chose to hold the ceremony in the grove, then the guests walked back to their cars and drove to a country restaurant for dinner.

Bob and Paula choose to get married in her parents' living room. It was just before her father retired, and her parents were soon going to sell the family home. By having her wedding at the house, Paula marked the completion of her childhood and the beginning of her marriage in a wonderfully symbolic way.

Don and Mary chose the small hotel with hot mineral springs where they had vacationed together. They gathered their dearest friends for an entire weekend of celebration and sharing. One friend led the group in yoga classes, another in creating a sculpture for the bride and groom, another in a moving community dialogue. The outdoor pool and sulfur springs encouraged people to drop their inhibitions and come into a heartful place. By bringing people together for an extended period of time, they created a beautifully bonded community that was there to shore them up with their blessing by the time the actual ceremony occurred.

Laura and Steve chose their own backyard. By simply looking out the window at the rose garden where they had spoken their vows, they wanted to be continually reminded of the promises they made to one another and, on difficult days, to imagine that their friends and family were still out there celebrating and encouraging.

Other potential locations include a private club, an art museum, a historical site, a botanical garden or vineyard, the chapel at a college or university, or the grounds of a beautiful public building such as the library or courthouse.

Once you've found a location you like, make sure you consider the size of the setting in relation to the kind of ceremony you're planning. Will your guests overflow an intimate chapel or be lost in a huge cathedral? If you have your heart set on inviting two hundred people, they won't all fit on your cousin's cabin cruiser. Of course, if location is more important to you than number of people, your choice of setting can help determine how many guests to invite.

Be sure to investigate all the practical considerations: What is the rental fee? Are there additional fees, such as for cleanup or security? Is there ample parking? Dressing rooms with lights and mirrors? Churches in particular may have dress codes; are there restrictions regarding attire, flowers, candles, decorations, or music? What equipment—sound system, extension cords, decorations, runners and canopies, kneeling cushions—is available, and what will you have to provide?

What is the policy regarding photography? Through whom are deliveries (flowers, musical equipment, gifts) coordinated? Is a

It is only necessary to know that love is a direction and not a state of the soul. If one is unaware of this, one falls into despair at the first onslaught of affliction.

—*Simone Weil*

rehearsal necessary for the ceremony? If so, when will it be held and how long will it take? Will there be any other ceremonies held there the same day? If so, how will conflicts be avoided?

If you are choosing an outdoor setting, what will you do if it rains? What about bugs? Sun? Will people stand and, if so, is the ceremony brief enough? Is it quiet or is there a lot of background noise—cars, airplanes, caterers clanking dishes in the next room?

If you're planning to hold both ceremony and reception in the same place, how will the ceremony end? In a church ceremony, the wedding party and guests all file out into a receiving line or on to the reception hall. But if the location requires that you stay in the same room as the wedding, what will you do? One possibility is to have the officiant declare at the end of the service, "I now invite you to come forward and congratulate the bride and groom."

❧ THE LIGHT IN YOUR CEREMONY ❧

Light, usually in the form of candles, has always played a significant part in the traditional wedding ceremony. Light is our essence; it inhabits us and we seek it—in all its manifestations. Light creates brilliance; it means illumination, the most profound knowing that we may ever achieve. It also refers to the sun—the source of light that sustains all life—and to the moon, the light of emotion, which is the inspiration for romance.

Thus, as you plan your wedding, you will want to be aware not only of the "lighting" of your ceremony—how the church or garden is actually illumined—but also of what additional light you choose to bring into it. Words are light to the mind; music is illumination to the spirit; light of the incandescent bulb and the flame are light to the eye and the inner eye, respectively.

In Ceremonial Flourishes, I have included some special rituals with candles; but you will also want to consider what, overall, is the role that you want light to play in your ceremony, and what is the message you wish to have conveyed by it? Do you want an outside ceremony, conducted under the afternoon sun, indicating that you are willing to submit your marriage to the scrutinizing light of day? Or do you want a nighttime, candlelit ceremony, emphasizing the mystery and the romance?

Would you like to have the entire congregation light small candles at a particular juncture of the ceremony (for example, just before you recite your vows), so your promises may seem to be made more vivid by the flood of light? Would you like to have each of your guests, upon entering the church (or meadow or synagogue), light a small candle which they can then leave at the entrance to greet you when you walk out as a married couple? Or to pass a single lighted candle from one to another until finally the officiant will install it (symbolically holding the flame of everyone's light) in a candlestick on the altar?

Would you each like to walk in with a candle (symbolizing your individual light), then ignite a single candle on the altar with the two of them? Or light candles together, symbolizing the illumination that is possible in union? Perhaps you would like each pew or row of chairs to be marked off by a candle, so that in entering the church the bride will walk down a pathway of light.

Light fills our souls with a sense of the infinite light. So enlighten yourselves, your guests, and your life, by flooding your wedding with light!

❧ MUSICAL CONSIDERATIONS ❧

Music has great power to draw us together, to touch us deep in our souls, at the place far beneath where language begins. In fact nothing, not even the setting, will do more to create the mood and spirit of your wedding.

The spoken portions of the ceremony will resonate their meanings to a higher and lovelier degree when they are set off by music. Music creates a meditative and reflective mood and, when juxtaposed with the spoken word, enables you and your guests to feel even more deeply the meanings of what is being said. Music is particularly effective as a kind of meditative punctuation after the readings, the address, and the exchanging of the vows.

Choose each musical selection as an expression of some unique aspect of your relationship, a reflection of something you've experienced together or of the hopes you hold for your marriage. There are, of course, numerous traditional wedding selections: the march from Lohengrin, the "Hawaiian Wedding Song," and "Promise Me." If these don't suit your fancy or reflect the depth of your feeling, or if they fail to create the kind of ambiance you have in mind, make your own selections. Don't be afraid to use something totally exceptional— a song you write or sing yourself, a Broadway show tune, something you heard on the radio last week, or your favorite Brahms intermezzo. Of course there are different musical genres—classical, popular, jazz. You may feel inclined to stick to one theme, but, again, allow the music to be a reflection of your feelings and your preferences.

Above all, the music should have meaning. If you know a singer, songwriter, composer, flautist, or guitar player, it would be lovely to include their original talent in your wedding. Don't be afraid to ask; it's an honor and a pleasure for most musicians to perform, even if they're not first-rate professionals. Let the love they express through their gift, and your love and appreciation for them, be a touching part of your ceremony.

Along with the music you include to delineate each step in the unfolding of your ceremony, consider beginning your wedding with a small concert or serenade. If you can, feature live music, although recorded music is fine, and can be a boon, especially if you're featuring a specific piece—an aria by Caruso, "your song" as a couple, or your favorite symphony. But, because you're looking for the heartfelt for all aspects of your wedding, if you can possibly arrange it, go for the real thing—the singer you know, a local harpist, the live piano performance.

Finally, be realistic. You probably don't have room for the New York Philharmonic. If that tiny chapel you've both decided is perfect doesn't have a pipe organ, be willing to settle for a piano or a string quartet. Also, check to make sure that whoever performs will actually have enough room to do so comfortably.

Let the music play on! Allow it to touch you, to bring you and your guests together, to be a magical veil of beautiful sounds that floats through your wedding like a breeze.

❧ TO REHEARSE OR NOT? ❧

Should you have a rehearsal? The answer really depends on you (and the advice of your officiant). If your ceremony involves several people, if you have very young attendants, or if you're feeling anxious about the choreography of the wedding or who will be doing what when, you should definitely schedule at least one rehearsal. The rehearsal can be quick and easy, a walk- and talk-through of each part of the wedding, with the bride and groom, all the attendants, the officiant, and the musician(s) all taking their places, practicing their movements, and being apprised of what each participant of the ceremony is supposed to be doing.

Usually by the time you've run through the ceremony twice—which you can probably do in an hour and a half—everyone will start to feel comfortable. If you go through each step of the ceremony on-site, you will discover whatever details still need to be dealt with: Is the bride clear about when and how she will enter? Who will hold the rings? the bride's bouquet? Who will manage her train, if there is one?

Everyone with a speaking part in the ceremony should be reminded to speak slowly, clearly, and loudly enough for everyone to hear. If they read too quickly or slowly, the beautiful pieces you've chosen won't have the impact you hoped for. Again, a public practice could be useful.

The rehearsal is also the time to discuss seating arrangements with the ushers: Will the bride's family be on the left and the groom's on the right? Or will people sit wherever they wish? If the bride's and groom's guests will be divided, assign the ushers to one side or another at this time.

Most couples think they won't be nervous at the ceremony, but often they're more nervous than they expect, anxious that everything will come off as scheduled. For some people it is the fear of speaking in public; for others it's being the center of attention. Oddly enough, though, it's this touch of tension that gives a wedding its emotional authenticity—the blushing bride and jittery groom reveal to each other and everyone else that this isn't just a performance. It's a heartfelt, life-changing occasion.

If you are afraid of speaking in public and all you want to do is silently stand there and say, "I do," you can still create a personalized wedding. Write out the pieces you want the officiant or others to say. And if you do want to say something yourself, I strongly suggest you have notes nearby; notes are a good security net. More than one couple has regretted not having a written reminder of the lines they worked so hard to perfect, and no one expects you to have it all memorized.

Also, be aware that due to nervousness, your fingers might swell. If you're having a ceremony with rings, you might have trouble placing them on each other's fingers. Being mindful of this will help you stay calm if you do have difficulty. In anticipation, you might just want to agree that instead of trying to put the rings on the appropriate fingers during the ceremony, you'll just slip them onto each other's pinkies until you've walked back down the aisle.

And if during the actual ceremony, people (including you) stand in the wrong spot, flub their lines, or enter in the wrong order, don't fret. You're there to celebrate your love, and it's the spirit you create through your ceremony that's what matters, not whether the flower girl forgot to throw the rose petals or the best man read the poem too quickly.

❧ THE REHEARSAL DINNER ❧ AND OTHER PRE-WEDDING FESTIVITIES

A rehearsal dinner is a celebration in itself. As hors d'oeuvres are to a meal, the rehearsal is the lighthearted prelude to the more serious main course of emotions that will follow. How ceremonial you want the rehearsal dinner to be will depend, of course, on what kind of wedding you're planning. If your wedding is small, a wedding-eve gathering of your two families and your attendants (and their partners) would constitute an intimate get-together that you could have at a restaurant or at the home of either the bride's or groom's parents.

Since the bride's family traditionally pays the wedding expenses, the groom's family usually underwrites the cost of the rehearsal dinner. That's a nice tradition to follow, but for any number of reasons you may want to vary it—pay for it yourselves, or, as in at least one instance I know of, accept it as the gift from the best man or a friend of the family.

For a grander, more formal wedding, you'll probably want to plan a larger, more elegant dinner with pre-wedding toasts, perhaps even a receiving line to introduce all family members. You may want to include the officiant and musicians, as well. Whatever the roster of guests, the rehearsal dinner is the time for you to give out the customary gifts or tokens you have provided for the members of your wedding party.

In general, the rehearsal dinner is a wedding send-off, a sort of private cheerleading for the big event. It's a way of boosting the energy so everyone can bring a high sense of expectation to the ceremony itself.

Of course, the rehearsal dinner is often replaced or accompanied by the "bachelor party," which can follow (or precede) the dinner and is a symbolic "final" gathering of the groom and male friends. At this event (the exact nature of which is determined by the participants—a barbecue, an all-night drinking party, a camp-out) the groom is, as it were, sent out, with a final rousing hurrah, from the male-only community. This is his rite of passage from the world of single men to that of marriage and life with a woman.

In addition, it is becoming more common for her women friends to create a special ceremony for the bride before the wedding. In such a ritual (and you can develop your own—a slumber party, a night out on the town, a water ceremony in the ocean or a pool) a woman is prepared by her sisters to leave the female community and embark upon life with a man.

❧ FINAL REMINDERS ❧

Remember to bring your marriage license to the wedding. The officiant can't marry you without it. Also, be sure you have the required number of witnesses and that the ceremony is performed within the time and place limits specified by your state; the dates and other legal requirements are usually stamped on the license. There's also a time limit within which the license must be filed. Be sure to take note of that too.

❧ POSTSCRIPT ❧

Taking everything into consideration, from the mundane to the sublime, you can create an amazingly beautiful wedding; the experience of planning it can be a wonderful opportunity for growth. As the two of you navigate the waves of stress and excitement that inevitably will be part of it, you'll discover a lot of things about each other that you never knew before—how your tastes differ and are similar, what you can and can't take for granted, which of your fuses blow for what reasons, how each of you is affected by the things you're choosing to include—and how your love carries you through.

In a sense, planning a wedding is the first test of a marriage. If you can move graciously through all the possible pitfalls—if you're willing to learn, if you face your conflicts and resolve them, if you stumble onto and are ignited again by a deep nostalgia about your love—the creation of your wedding will be more than just your first major joint undertaking, it, too, can truly be a gift of love.

the
CEREMONIAL
ELEMENTS

From the most common traditional wedding ceremonies, I have selected the fourteen elements that I believe have the most meaning for couples today. They are: the procession, the convocation, the invocation, the readings, the address, the consecration, the expression of intent, the vows, the blessing and exchanging of the rings, the pronouncement of marriage, the kiss, the benediction, and the recession.

You'll notice that I have not included, among other things, the "giving away" of the bride or the infamous "If anyone present has objections to this union, speak now or forever hold your peace." Both of these traditions spring from outdated notions, one viewing a woman as her father and/or husband's property, the other granting to the community the right of conferring the ultimate approval of a marriage. Neither of these is in keeping with the belief that marriage is a bond of freedom, a truly democratic enterprise, so I have therefore eliminated them. Of course, if you choose to include either of these conventions in your ceremony, you can insert them in the appropriate place among the elements presented here.

Also, many weddings include a celebration of the Mass or Holy Communion; but since these are very specific, both in content and in form, I suggest you use the order of service from your church if you choose to incorporate the Eucharist sacrament in your marriage ceremony. Your minister or priest can tell you where they belong.

What you should remember above all is that the entire wedding ceremony is a process of spiritual movement. Through its very format it leads us from a general to an ever more specific level of emotional involvement. It begins with a gathering together of the community and then, through a progression of words and music, directs our focus ever more intently upon the couple until, in the reciting of their vows, we witness their most intimate conversation.

Bearing this in mind, you will want to choose the components of your ceremony with great care, for the truly moving wedding service will sequentially move all those who witness it from outside themselves—what they were doing this morning, what they must do tomorrow—and draws them very intimately into the presence of the love that you two share. Understanding the purpose of each element will help you decide what to include and what you would prefer to omit.

❧ THE PROCESSION ❧

The traditional wedding march is one of the few remaining forms of procession we have today. A procession, by its very nature, symbolizes progress, a moving on from one state of being to another. In a procession one or more people move physically forward, ordinarily to music, representing the change that is occurring in them and carrying all those who witness it from one state of awareness to another.

In the procession of the wedding ceremony, we are all "moved" emotionally from an awareness of the bride and groom as individuals to one of a couple who are joined and then turn to face us in their union. They literally approach one another from a physical location which symbolizes their separate histories. We then see them come closer and closer through the exhortation, vows, exchanging of the rings, and finally the kiss that seals their union.

In the entire movement of the wedding, we see the symbolism of the bride moving from her past (her early life, her relationship with her parents) into the moment where she is first witnessed (symbolizing the falling in love), then approached by the groom (symbolizing his choosing, pursuing of her), until they stand together at the altar. Then they both move forward into an intimate teaching circle with the officiant, where the nature, obligations, and privileges of marriage are discussed, and promises of the future are expressed as they recite their wedding vows.

Whether we are consciously aware of it or not, it is this actual physical movement that carries us emotionally, step by step, through all the nuances of meaning in the ceremony. We all move, with the bride and groom, from recognizing their singleness to celebrating their union.

Because the bridal procession is the kinesthetic expression of this meaning, you will want to consider precisely what it is you would like to convey through this part of the ceremony. Do you want to emphasize the moving away from your parents and into the new relationship with your soon-to-be husband or wife? And would you, the bride, like your father to walk you down the aisle? Does your past or recent relationship with him merit it? Would a brother or friend be more appropriate? Or is there someone else whom you would prefer to accompany you, even if the choice is unconventional? Perhaps you would like to emphasize your individuality by walking down the aisle by yourself. Would you like to approach each other from opposite sides, signifying that in marriage you join one another across the distance of your separateness?

Celia, whose father died when she was a child, was escorted down the aisle by her ex-husband. In spite of their "irreconcilable differences," they were good friends, and he was the man who, above all, she believed, had truly prepared her for her present happiness. Jane was accompanied by her best woman friend, the person who had been closest to her for more than a decade. At her second marriage, Eileen, a widow, wanted to walk down the aisle with her children; they had shared her grief, and now she wanted them to share her joy. It was their love that had sustained her.

You should note that in the traditional Jewish ceremony, both the bride's and groom's parents accompany them to the altar. You may want to do something similar for reasons of your own—because your wedding strongly symbolizes the coming together of two families, or because you're both close to your parents and want to honor them.

Apart from all these special variations, most wedding processions generally follow the pattern of either the Christian or the Jewish tradition, both of which are described in detail in Additional Selections. Although you may want to depart from these and create a unique processional choreography of your own, it's good to know the standard procedures, what they symbolize, and, therefore, what any departure from them may be seen to express.

❧ THE CONVOCATION ❧

The convocation consists of the words spoken to commence the wedding. This is the ceremonial gathering together of the bride and groom with the family and friends they have chosen to share the occasion. Here the guests are called upon to note what is about to transpire and to create a ceremonial halo of love around the bride and groom.

The intent behind this part of the ceremony is to demonstrate not only that you are affirming your love to each other, but also that you believe in it so strongly that you want to express your hopes, your expectations, and your commitment in the presence of these witnesses.

What is also being acknowledged is that the people attending your wedding are not mere observers chewing popcorn in the grand-stands; by their very presence they are bearing high witness and setting a seal of approval on your marriage. Their attendance confirms the reality of your intentions. The fact that they shared this most important event with you will stand to support you through all the days of your marriage. It is the convocation that calls them to this privilege.

❧ THE INVOCATION ❧

These are the words through which you call on God, or whatever outside, higher, or more radiant presence you choose to acknowledge and bear witness to your ceremony. The purpose of the invocation is to put you and your guests into a more meditative and reflective frame of mind, to focus your attention on the fact that what you are undertaking is serious, life-changing, and powerful. It also asks you to contemplate whom or what you will call upon as your comforter, source, and highest witness as you walk the path of marriage. For many, this higher presence is God; for others, it is the highest dimension of their own selves.

Whatever power you choose to invoke here, the invocation invites you to put yourself in the presence of the holy, to acknowledge that as a couple you stand in relationship to all that is. The invocation acknowledges that you are sanctifying your relationship not only to one another but also in the presence of the divine; it invites you to take your place, through marriage, in the human stream.

Aloneness and connection are like tides in the sea of your heart, separate tides, flowing in and out.

—M. C. Richards

❧ THE READINGS ❧

In this part of the ceremony the officiant, one or more friends, or you, yourself, reads the selections you have made from this book or other sources. The readings are designed to inspire contemplation, to invite you and your witnesses to expand your views about love and marriage. I have included some selections from the Bible, the classics, and various other sources, but you may want to make selections of your own.

The purpose of the readings is to introduce into your ceremony reflections on the meaning of love and marriage that have spoken to people over the ages or that say something of particular significance to you. If you make a selection from the classics, you will be choosing words that have been used at myriad nuptial celebrations and which carry the rich legacy of having moved the hearts of many lovers. Thus in using them, in hearing them spoken at your wedding, you will bind yourselves to the great tradition of marriage and to the celebrations of husbands and wives from other times and other places.

If you'd rather be more personal, however, choose your own favorite poem, the words on a card you once sent him, a love letter she tucked under your pillow. The point is that the selection should reveal something particular about you two. By having such a personal selection read aloud, you open a door for your witnesses, inviting them into the intimate magic of your union. In any case, the readings provide an opportunity to reflect on the many meanings of love and commitment, and generally introduce the theme that will be revealed in the next portion of the wedding.

❧ THE ADDRESS ❧

The address, frequently called the homily or sermon, constitutes a message of celebration and exhortation by the officiant at your ceremony, the person you have chosen to teach and inspire you, to set the cornerstone of meaning for the new life you are entering. The purpose of the officiant's address is twofold: to deliver a message directed to you personally, and to inspire in your guests a deep sense of the meaning of love and the value of marriage.

This is an opportunity for you to add some dimension to your wedding, to have someone express what you truly feel about the meaning of marriage. Therefore, in planning the address with your officiant, you will want to bring to his or her attention not only what is important to you about your relationship thus far, but also what you hope to accomplish by getting married.

While it is traditional for the officiant to give his or her own sermon, I am including these addresses because they enable you to contemplate the landscape of marriage through a variety of lenses, and to direct the officiant toward the particular view that you want expressed. The addresses offered here are brief and specifically focus on particular aspects of marriage. You may ask your officiant to use them as a springboard, or you may wish to have one of them read in its entirety, to serve as part or all of the address.

If you prefer to give your officiant free rein with the address, you may want to use a selection from any address or from *Reflections on Marriage* as one of the readings in your ceremony.

❧ THE CONSECRATION ❧

The words of the consecration follow the address and serve to underline and elevate the message you have just heard. To consecrate means to make holy, and in this section of the ceremony, the officiant once again draws attention to your exalted undertaking. Having heard the words of inspiration and instruction, you now prepare to make the promises that will express your desire to fulfill the meaning of marriage as it has been expressed in the address.

Whether of exhortation or of prayer, the words of the consecration remind you that what you are undertaking is sacred. They charge you to give serious attention to the commitment you are about to make. They also serve as a transition from the teaching and exhorting part of the ceremony to the more intimate phase in which you make your promises to one another. They bridge those parts of the ceremony that are shared equally by celebrants, to focus attention directly on the individuals getting married.

❧ THE EXPRESSION OF INTENT ❧

Here you are invited to make public your desire to wed. Having heard about the challenges, demands, and joys of marriage in the previous portions of the ceremony, you now state publicly that you intend to go forward with the making of your promises. Like the consecration, the expression of intent calls your attention to the seriousness of the promises you are about to make, the state you are about to enter into. But here, rather than being instructed, encouraged, or forewarned, you acknowledge aloud your intention to go forward.

❧ THE VOWS ❧

The vows, of course, are the part we remember most about any wedding ceremony. Your vows are the emotionally and spiritually binding part of the ceremony. Vows are love made tangible. They both reach from and speak to the heart. They advertise the love that brought you together, and draw a blueprint for the love you intend to sustain.

Your vows are more than a bouquet of pretty words spoken in the presence of your witnesses. They are your heartfelt spoken promises of what you are willing to do for one another, under what circumstances, and for what length of time. As you speak these words, you are making yourself accountable through intention—to yourself and to your beloved—to live, love, and behave in certain specified ways. Regardless of whether in time you are able to live up to your vows to perfection, what you say here is of the utmost importance; for spoken and witnessed, these words will continuously call you to the emotional, behavioral, and spiritual commitment that from this day forward you are choosing to undertake.

The vows offered here represent both an expansion and a revision of the traditional vows, in that they include some very specific promises about the nature of the union you are entering into. They are tailored to the particular kinds of ceremonies presented here. Once again, you may want to use them exactly as they are written here, or as a basis for formulating your own vows.

In either case, I suggest that during the ceremony you consider reading them in their entirety instead of repeating them after the officiant. You may want to write them out in advance and carry them with you, or have one of your attendants hand them to you at the appropriate time. Reading them yourselves will more deeply connect you to their meaning, and, because you are making these promises in the presence of witnesses, they will take on even greater significance.

I also suggest that when you say your vows, you turn directly toward one another and recite them face-to-face, instead of facing the officiant. You'll be amazed by the effect that expressing your promises directly to each other can have on the bonds you are making, as well as by the intense feeling this soul-to-soul encounter will arouse in you both.

Because the vows are such a precious and important part of the wedding, at the back of this book I have also included several additional vows that you may be inspired by and prefer to use.

❧ THE BLESSING AND EXCHANGING ❧ OF THE RINGS

Wedding rings are the material symbol of the bond that is created in marriage. Because you will wear your rings from your wedding day onward, the words spoken about them and, consequently, the meaning they will embody as a result of your ceremony, is of the greatest importance. More than anything else in your wedding, the rings are what you will take with you. The flowers will wilt, and the reception will end, but your wedding ring will be there to remind you day after day that you are loved, that you have been chosen.

Therefore you will want to ensure that the blessing spoken by the officiant and the words you choose to speak at the time you exchange your rings express most purely the meaning you want to live with every day you wear them.

❧ THE PRONOUNCEMENT OF MARRIAGE ❧

The pronouncement of marriage is the public proclamation that you are married, and the presentation by the officiant of you as husband and wife. This is a lovely and special moment, the archway of words through which you now reenter the community. No longer solitary, but formally bonded to one another, you have passed through the portal to married life.

❧ THE KISS ❧

Need I say more? This is the delicious part of the ceremony, the moment in which you claim one another with a kiss.

The kiss seals the promise. The kiss signifies reverence. Traditionally a kiss confers not only greeting and honor but also attachment. One salutes and claims whomever he or she kisses, so the kiss is more than a delightful public display of the physical affections that complement the marriage; it is the way in which the groom claims the bride as his forevermore, the way in which the bride claims the groom as forever hers.

❧ THE BENEDICTION ❧

The benediction is the final ceremonial flourish of the wedding. With these words, you, the newly married couple, are sent off with a blessing to halo your union through the long days of the future. The benediction is buoyant; it offers you good wishes, mirth, joy, exuberance, and maybe one final fillip of exhortation as you set sail for the world.

This is a brief but delightful and rousing moment, the climax of all the excitement, seriousness, and loveliness that has been unfolding in the marriage ceremony. It should be joyous, boisterous, exuberant, and should be followed immediately by jubilant recessional music.

❦ THE RECESSION ❧

Just as the processional process carries much rich symbolism and leads us, literally step by step, into the wedding ceremony, so the recession also conveys deep meaning. The spirit of the recession is one of joy and jubilation. The bride and groom are together at last; they have secured their bond and sealed it with a kiss; they are ready to go out, united, into the world.

In the recession those who have served the bride and groom in helping them to get married—their parents, attendants, and the officiant himself—all follow them out. Now the bride and groom lead the way. They represent the frontier of love, the radiant future.

The traditional format for the recession is as follows: When the spoken service is completed, the organist or musicians start playing joyful recessional music; the bride and groom walk down the aisle; the flower girl and ring-bearer (the next generation of bride and groom) immediately follow. Then the maid of honor and each of the bridesmaids, accompanied by the best man and ushers, respectively, recess down the aisle, followed by the bride's, then the groom's, mother and father. Finally, to the concluding strains of recessional music, the entire congregation walks out.

❦ A SELECTION OF CEREMONIES ❧

Because a wedding is one of those rare opportunities we have to experience ritual in our lives, it is very important that you create a wedding that symbolizes exactly what you want it to. A wedding is an encounter with the extraordinary, in the midst of ordinary life, that truly elevates our spirits and brings us into the presence of the holy. Weddings remind us that our lives have meaning and that love is the strongest bond, the happiest joy, and the loveliest healing we can ever experience. It is these notions that form the heart of the ceremonies here, but each ceremony also carries an individual emphasis, a special point of view.

That's because there are a great many aspects to the commitment of marriage. Exactly what you want your wedding to express will depend on your circumstances and your history, your values and your intentions, your view of life, and your beliefs about relationships. Your wedding is the single most special opportunity you will ever have to say to each other, in the company of people who love you, just how much your relationship means to you, and what path you are laying out for your future. So as you go about planning your wedding, I suggest that you read through all of these ceremonies before making your final selection. See which one seems to capture the mood and point of view that best communicate what you want to express, then use or adapt it so that it becomes truly expressive of your own feelings and philosophy.

The popular notion about marriage and love is that they are synonymous, that they spring from the same motives, and cover the same human needs. Like most popular notions this also rests not on actual facts, but on superstition.

—*Emma Goldman*

The first wedding, which I am calling *The Marriage of Love and Commitment,* is a revision of the traditional Christian ceremony that acknowledges God as the author of love and the architect of the spiritual commitment of marriage. Here, revised, it offers the recipe for a sacred union expressed in a more contemporary form, keeping to the spiritual values but expressing them in more modern language.

The second ceremony, *The Marriage of Love and Purpose,* focuses on the psychological meanings of marriage. It acknowledges that in choosing our partners and in coming together in matrimony we make no mistake, that we build relationships to heal our emotional wounds and to lead ourselves toward the fulfillment of the highest purposes in our lives.

The third ceremony, *The Marriage of Love and Rejoicing,* is for the ecstatic and lighthearted among us who want to express in an exuberant, spontaneous, and perhaps less conventional manner their inestimable joy at finding their own true love. The spirit of this ceremony is lighter, sweeter; this ceremony easily adapts to an outdoor mountaintop wedding, a wedding on the Staten Island Ferry, in your artist friend's loft, or your own backyard.

The fourth ceremony, *The Marriage of Love and Fulfillment,* is designed especially for those who have been married before. When we marry a second (or third, or even fourth) time, we recognize that we have been brought to this place of fulfillment by everything that has gone on before. And either specifically or in a general way, we honor both where we've come from and where we are headed.

In addition, we instinctively want to create a ceremony that separates us from a mere repeat of the marriage (or marriages) we had before, the marriage(s) that didn't last till our death. We want to dignify, clarify, and celebrate the uniqueness of the present union and the hopes we hold for it. We want to create a ceremony that will allow us to believe afresh that this marriage is a true bond, that this ceremony honors a profound relationship that has a firm foothold in the future.

Then I have included a ceremony for those who are in recovery from an addiction. *The Marriage of Love and Renewal* is a special celebration for those to whom marriage is one of the highest rewards of a serious commitment to the process of self-healing. This ceremony acknowledges the suffering and uniqueness of that difficult past and celebrates with joy the love that is the legitimate birthright of its future.

Finally, at the conclusion of these ceremonies, for reference and resource, I have included three traditional services, aspects of which you may wish to include in any of the ceremonies here. But if you want to depart from custom and create a wedding uniquely your own, you may prefer to use one of the preceding new ceremonies, or incorporate selections exclusively from them.

Once again, you can use any ceremony verbatim, or mix and match elements as you like. However you arrange it, my sincerest wish for you is that you will have the wedding of your dreams, a wedding from your heart.

a SELECTION *of* CEREMONIES

THE MARRIAGE OF LOVE
AND COMMITMENT

𝕿

AMONG ITS MANY DIMENSIONS, MARRIAGE IS A spiritual enterprise, for the highest spiritual purpose of marriage is the embodiment of love; and love, as we know, is the strongest power there is. Love can truly change the world. Because we are so well acquainted with the emotional and social aspects of marriage, we often overlook its loftier dimensions. Yet it is because at some level we do sense that love is the true essence of marriage that we make our weddings such special events, and in our unconscious myths we hold marriage to be the most significant bond we can ever make.

Recognizing this at least intuitively, we know that we are called to marriage by no mistake, to participate in it as a gift in service not only to the fulfillment of the highest purposes in ourselves, but also to the creation of a loving union. We sense that the real meanings of marriage lie far beyond the specific tasks that we will undertake in it, even beyond what we create in one another through it. Through marriage we invite the development of our highest spiritual selves, that which is transcendent in us, that which participates in the pure experience of love.

In this spiritual view, marriage is the human union that replicates and symbolizes the relationship of God to humans, of love ethereal and eternal to life temporal and material. In holding these meanings for us, marriage invites us to examine our deepest beliefs, not only about relationships, but also about the power of love itself. It encourages us to allow our relationships to embody the highest values we can hold.

❧ THE CONVOCATION ❧

We are gathered here in the presence of God and of this company to join in holy marriage _____ and _____ and to bear witness to the transforming power of love.

Love is a quality of spirit and an attitude of the emotions, but a marriage is a life's work, a spiritual art form. Therefore, this is an occasion of both profound joy and great responsibility, and we who partake in it bind ourselves as witnesses to the labor of love that _____ and _____ are undertaking here.

In acknowledgment of this holy purpose and of the power of this occasion, let us pray.

❧ THE INVOCATION ❧

God of Light, who gives us the longing for love and the capability of loving, we give you thanks for _____ and _____, for their open hearts and willing spirits, and for the example of love that they embody here in our presence.

Be with them on this joyous occasion of showing their love and making their vows; and be with us, their witnesses, that we may all be changed by what is said and witnessed here.

❧ THE READINGS ❧

Colossians 3:12–14

Put on then, as God's chosen ones, holy and beloved, compassion, kindness, lowliness, meekness, and patience, forbearing one another, and, if one has a complaint against another, forgiving each other; as the Lord has forgiven you, so you must also forgive. And above all these put on love, which binds everything together in perfect harmony.

Sonnet 116

Let me not to the marriage of true minds
Admit impediments; love is not love
Which alters when it alteration finds,
Or bends with the remover to remove.
Oh no! It is an ever-fixed mark
That looks on tempests and is never shaken;
It is the star to every wand'ring bark,
Whose worth's unknown, although his height be taken.
Love's not Time's fool, though rosy lips and cheeks
Within his bending sickle's compass come;
Love alters not with its brief hours and weeks,
But bears it out even to the edge of doom.
If this be error and upon me proved,
I never writ, nor no man ever loved.
                              —*William Shakespeare*

1 Corinthians 13

Though I speak with the tongues of men and of angels, and have not charity, I am become as sounding brass, or a tinkling cymbal.

And though I have the gift of prophecy, and all knowledge; and though I have all faith so that I could remove mountains, and have not charity, I am nothing.

And though I bestow all my goods to feed the poor, and though I give my body to be burned, and have not charity, it profiteth me nothing.

Charity suffereth long, and is kind; charity envieth not; charity vaunteth not itself, is not puffed up,

Doth not behave itself unseemly; seeketh not her own, is not easily provoked, thinketh no evil;

Rejoiceth not in iniquity, but rejoiceth in the truth;

Beareth all things, believeth all things, hopeth all things, endureth all things.

Charity never faileth: but whether there be prophecies, they shall fail; whether there be tongues, they shall cease; whether there be knowledge, it shall vanish away.

For we know in part, and we prophesy in part.

But when that which is perfect is come, then that which is in part shall be done away.

When I was a child I spake as a child, I understood as a child, I thought as a child; but when I became a man, I put away childish things.

For now we see through a glass darkly; but then face to face: now I know in part; but then shall I know even as also I am known.

And now abideth faith, hope, charity, these three; but the greatest of these is charity.

❧ THE ADDRESS ❧

We are gathered here to celebrate a marriage, a spiritual union that embodies love's most profound possibilities. Saint Paul, the author of this letter to the Corinthians, uses the word charity to refer to the highest form of love that we can ever ask of ourselves. As we have heard in these readings, love in this form is the greatest of virtues; love is the highest spiritual work. Love is both immanent and transcendent. And it is love, kindled by romance and clasped by heartfelt marriage vows, that has the capacity to deliver marriage from being merely a domestic arrangement, a supportive partnership, and an emotional bonding, and elevate it into a spiritual enterprise.

To speak of marriage as a spiritual enterprise is to view it in a slightly different way than normally, and certainly not simply in a romantic light. For when we speak of marriage in spiritual terms, we are inviting ourselves into it—and it into us—at a much higher level. To participate in a marriage of this kind is not only to enter into it as the estate that will bring us happiness, but to see it also as the spiritual crucible of transformation, of suffering, and also of great joy.

Therefore, as you step into marriage you must remember first of all that marriage is a process of transformation. Because of it, inside of it, and in response to it, you will change most remarkably. And not necessarily or exclusively in the ways you had hoped for or imagined. For marriage is the spiritual grinding stone that will hone you to your brightest brilliance. It will cause you to become not only who you wanted to be, but also the person whom you have no choice but to be. In marriage you will be re-formed, for in choosing this particular person to love and make your whole life with, you are choosing to be affected. You will be polished through the actions of your beloved upon you, through the praise, criticism, frustration, excitement, actions, and inactions of the person you marry today.

In this regard it is important to remember that, more than you can possibly imagine, you are unconsciously drawn to precisely that person who possesses the attributes you need to be affected by in order to change. These are the very qualities which, because of their capacity to irritate and inspire you, will encourage in you the very dimensions you lack, the qualities which, as you acquire them, will represent an enlargement of your soul. What this means, simply, is that in spite of yourself you will be drawn into a process of personal evolution. Whatever is missing in your character will gradually be developed, and what's remarkable about this transformation is that in the end, rather than feeling bitter, resentful, or unwilling, you will come to see the acquisition of these attributes as an exquisite refinement of your spirit.

This is a spiritual process because it deals not with the superficial aspects of your personality—how you dress and what you eat, although changes in these areas may also be part of the process—but with the deepest essence of your being and, ultimately, with your capacity to love. You will learn to be kinder, or more gently critical, to be empathetic, or more trusting. For wherever we are bound by our own emotional limitations, wherever we have judgments or cannot come into the presence of our own generosity or compassion because of our woundedness, there, certainly, we will be met in marriage. We will be met in the character of our beloved, with an invitation to transcend our own limitations—our judgments, our stinginess, our lack of trust, our fear of intimacy, our pride, our self-focus, our self-righteousness—and strive for their beautiful opposites, to reach, in short, for our capacity to love.

For it is love, of course, true love, unconditional love, the love of the tree for the earth, the love of the bird for the air, the love of God for creation, that shatters all limitations, that dissolves all fears. This unconditional love is the true gift of marriage, its greatest, most spirit-embracing work.

As marriage will change us and develop in us the true power of our love, so also will it call us to the highest labors of that love. First Corinthians 13, for example, talks about the specific qualities of love that allow us to develop as spirits. It tells us that along with bearing, believing, hoping, and enduring, "love suffers long." So we are being instructed through this ancient writing that love isn't only the roses and romance that bring us to the altar, but that it includes, more formidably, the quality that Saint Paul calls "suffering." This sounds difficult, certainly not something that would entice us into marriage; so what, exactly, do we mean by "suffering"?

Among its many meanings are: "to undergo, to experience, to pass through, to endure without sinking . . . to allow, to permit, to not forbid or hinder"; also, "to tolerate, to put up with." Thus, when Corinthians says that love suffers long, it does not mean that love is masochistic or foolish, but that love is generous, brave, creative, enduring, adventurous, and strong.

Through such contemplation, we are being invited to move beyond the romantic view of marriage and encounter the truth that in marriage love does, indeed, "suffer" in all these meanings of the word—and to a most remarkable degree. For it is in the nature of love to participate, to undergo—and not as an exception, but as the rule. Love calls upon us, not only for the sake of our beloved but also in the service of love itself, to constantly expand our reach, to become much more than we are.

Thus in what we will bear, go through, endure without sinking, or just plain put up with, marriage encourages us to the ultimate expansion of our capabilities. It is in this way that love invites us into the state of spiritual evolution which requires that, on behalf of our beloved, we pass again and again through what we believe are our own limitations, that over and over we accept the seemingly unacceptable and endure what we believe we cannot endure.

To know that marriage has a high spiritual purpose is to be willing to bear the sufferings that lie along its path. But it is also to rejoice and be glad, to be exuberant and playful, to bask in the companionship of the person who delights you, to participate in the joys of incarnation by being happy animals, creatures of passion and habit and comfort.

For marriage as a spiritual enterprise is also, in essence, about joy. It is joy that brings us to marriage, joy that inhabits its happiest moments, and joy with which we shall contemplate it when our lives draw to a close. For it is the joy of all joy, the infinite joy, which in its finite form a marriage symbolizes. For joy, unlike happiness, which is merely an emotion, is a state of being—that state of ultimate bliss and intimate union in which nothing and no one is separate from anything or anyone. In joy are we born; to joy we shall return. Joy is an endless ecstatic state, the ultimate spiritual condition.

To suffer the challenges of marriage is also to deliver yourself to its joys—to joy itself. And it is thus, in the spirit of joy, that we welcome ____ and ____ to the spiritual undertaking that is marriage. Long may it stand as the cathedral of their love.

❧ THE CONSECRATION ❧

Dear God, look mercifully upon your children, ____ and ____, and be generous with them, so that in the unfolding veils of time, they may truly stand for one another as emblems of the incarnation of your love. Give them a sense of joy, excitement, possibility, and challenge about what they are undertaking here, the ever-unfolding and beautiful work of refining their spirits in the presence of each other's witness, of becoming the bearers of your love.

And knowing that this is a high and often difficult work— that its rewards are uncommon, invisible—often, in ordinary day-to-day life, we pray for them the benediction of company, the encouragement of witnesses, the boundless joy of living always in the midst of love.

Give them peace of heart and strength of spirit so they may honor the vows they make here today. And may the promises they make inspire and instruct each one of us who celebrates with them. Amen.

❧ THE EXPRESSION OF INTENT ❧

Now that you have heard the high calling of marriage, do you ____ choose ____ to be your honored and cherished wife (husband/partner/mate), to live with her (him) and love her (him) in the consecrated state of marriage?

Answer: I do choose to marry her (him).

❧ THE VOWS ❧

In the name of God, I, ____, take you, ____, to be
my beloved wife (husband/mate), to have you and hold you,
to honor you, to treasure you,

to be at your side in sorrow and in joy
to suffer with you and to be transformed,
and to love and cherish you always.

I promise you this from my heart, with my soul,
for all the days of my life,
and, if God wills,
beyond the walls of life,
beyond the bounds of time.

THE BLESSING OF THE RINGS

As God is a circle whose center is everywhere and whose circumference is nowhere, so let the seamless circle of these rings become the symbol of your endless love.

THE EXCHANGING OF THE RINGS

Beloved ____, I give you this ring
as a symbol of my steadfastness and joy
in loving you, and as a pledge to honor you
with all that I am and all I shall become
for my whole life.

THE PRONOUNCEMENT OF MARRIAGE

Now that you, ____, and you, ____, have promised to give yourselves to one another and to love each other through your sacred vows and through the giving and receiving of these rings, I now pronounce you husband and wife (married).
Those whom God has joined together may he generously bless forever. You may now kiss one another.

❧ THE KISS ❧

❧ THE BENEDICTION ❧

Because you can rest in the comfort of knowing that you are chosen through one another to serve the highest purposes of love, depart in peace, recognizing that what you undertake together will bring you inestimable joy, and that the love you share can truly help to change the world. Now go forth from this place with jubilation in your hearts and gladness in your feet. Amen.

THE MARRIAGE OF LOVE
AND PURPOSE

THIS CEREMONY SEES MARRIAGE AS A CELEBRATION
of human destiny. It acknowledges that the union will have as one of
its major commitments the willingness of the partners to search for,
discover, and support one another as they step into the presence of
what is theirs, truly, to do in this life.

Couples who are drawn to this ceremony are those to whom their
own psychological development and emotional healing are of para-
mount importance in their lives. They have a sense of destiny, indeed
of urgency, about discovering who they are and what, in some ultimate sense, their lives are about.

Of course we don't all always consciously know the direction our
lives are taking, or how the person to whom we are attracted fits
into this process. We may know simply that we have fallen in love and
find ourselves getting married. If your purposes are as clear to you as
you might imagine they could be from the words of this wedding,
or simply if you are open to discovering them, this particular ceremony
assumes that you approach your lives from the point of view that
life is purposeful.

Some people have already set themselves on the path of discovering what their life purpose is, and they see their beloved as being
as intricately related to the fulfillment of their own destiny as they are
to the fulfillment of their partner's. If you are a couple who operate
from this perspective, you have already been asking yourselves a lot
of questions about who you are and what you intend to do with your
life. You have already made knowing yourselves a high priority. In
keeping with these values, as you contemplate the celebration of your

wedding, you will want to consider carefully what it is that you wish to say and have said at this, the ceremonial portal to the fulfillment of your common and individual purposes.

Therefore, you will want to ask yourself not only what you desire to receive from your union in support of your own destiny, but also what the two of you together, in the particular and unique configuration of your marriage, have been brought together to accomplish. What is your own personal destiny? What is your common life about? What, through your union, can you develop and nurture in one another? Where, in the present and the long future, do you as a couple mean to go? How can you go there beautifully and what part does your partner play in the process of your mutual and individual unfolding?

Asking and answering these questions as you plan your wedding will allow you to create a ceremony that truly reflects the highest values you hold for your lives. Then, just as the arrow strung in the bow is already poised for its highest destination, so your wedding ceremony shall become the moment in which you set the loftiest purposes of your life in motion.

❧ THE CONVOCATION ❧

____ and ____, Mr. and Mrs. (names of the bride's parents), Mr. and Mrs. ____ (names of the groom's parents), beloved friends, colleagues, accomplices, witnesses, we have come here to celebrate the marriage and the intertwining of destinies of ____ and ____, who, through being ruthlessly and wonderfully themselves, have fallen in love and chosen to get married.

Whether we know it or not, the path of our lives is already laid out deep within us, and life is the process of being willing to discover the direction of our path, the giving of ourselves to whatever it takes to be able to hit the mark. In other words, we are all here for a reason, and it is our business, as our lives progress, not only to discover what that purpose is but also to cultivate the conditions—whether emotional, educational, personal, or geographic—that allow us to fulfill that highest purpose.

In this context, marriage is a nurturing matrix in which two individuals can continue to expand and develop, so they can fulfill their individual destinies and offer their gifts to life and to the world. In this view, the focus is not so much on the couple and what they may undertake together, but more on the power of the individuals and what they have to contribute through their lives, how their union serves to enlarge and develop each of them.

Although this may appear on the surface to be an unromantic vision of love, it is a view that holds a relationship in the highest spiritual regard, for it has as its underlying assumption that each of us is alive for an important purpose, and that marriage enhances that capacity for individual contribution and participation.

_____ and _____ have stretched their individual development so far that they are no longer laboring alone to become themselves, but have arrived at the point in self-discovery where they can offer themselves as accomplices of destiny to one another.

It is in this spirit that they marry, not just because of their ineffable attraction to one another, but because the composite of their experiences has brought them to the place where they are ready to fulfill what is theirs to accomplish in this life, to join the forces of their individual spirits, capabilities, and backgrounds for the purpose of accomplishing together and individually what is theirs to do.

Therefore, we celebrate with them their arrival at the portal of true and conscious loving. We are incredibly happy for them and with them that one of the landmarks in the vast landscape of their becoming is the love that has brought them, and us, to the joyous occasion of this marriage.

You've been somebody long enough. You spent the first half of your life becoming somebody. Now you can work on becoming nobody, which is really somebody. For when you become nobody there is no tension, no pretense, no one trying to be anyone or anything. The natural state of the mind shines through unobstructed—and the natural state of the mind is pure love.

—*Ram Dass*

✎ THE INVOCATION ✎

All-knowing spirit in whose presence all human spirits bend to their becoming, we invite, indeed we entreat, you to join us in this ceremony binding the lives and destinies of ____ and ____. As they speak and we hear the words that will forever join them, allow the intentions being uttered in their hallowed conversation to stand true in time and run deep as a singing river through the landscape of their lives.

✎ THE READINGS ✎

In Love Made Visible

In love are we made visible
As in a magic bath
are unpeeled
to the sharp pit
so long concealed

With love's alertness
we recognize
the soundless whimper
of the soul
behind the eyes
A shaft opens
and the timid thing
at last leaps to surface
with full-spread wing

The fingertips of love discover
more than the body's smoothness
They uncover a hidden conduit
for the transfusion
of empathies that circumvent
the mind's intrusion

In love are we set free
Objective bone
and flesh no longer insulate us
to ourselves alone
We are released
and flow into each other's cup
Our two frail vials pierced
drink each other up
                    —*May Swenson*

A Vision

Two angels among the throng of angels
paused in the upward abyss,
facing angel to angel.

Blue and green glowed the wingfeathers
of one angel, from red to gold the sheen
of the other's. These two,

so far as angels may dispute, were poised
on the brink of dispute, brink of
fall from angelic stature,

for these tall ones, angels
whose wingspan encompasses entire
earthly villages, whose heads if their feet touched earth

would top pines or redwoods, live by their vision's harmony
which sees at one glance
the dark and light of the moon.

These two hovered dazed before one another,
for one saw the seafeathered, peacock breakered
crests of the other angel's magnificence,
different from his own,

and the other's eyes flickered with vision of
flame petallings, cream-gold grainfeather glitterings,
the wings of his fellow,
and both in immortal danger of dwindling, of dropping
into the remote forms of a lesser being.

But as these angels, the only halted ones
among the many who passed and repassed,
trod air as swimmers tread water, each gazing

on the angelic wings of the other,
the intelligence proper to great angels flew into their wings,
the intelligence called intellectual love, which,
understanding the perfections of scarlet,

leapt up among blues and greens strongshafted,
and among amber down illumined the sapphire bloom,

so that each angel was iridescent with the strange newly-seen
hues he watched; and their discovering pause
and the speech their silent interchange of perfection was

never became a shrinking to opposites,

and they remained free in the heavenly chasm,
remained angels, but dreaming angels,
each imbued with the mysteries of the other.
—*Denise Levertov*

❧ THE ADDRESS ❧

_____ and _____, you are here because separately and for a long time
you have each chosen the path of self-knowledge. You have paid
attention to who you are, what your life means, and where you are
going. But today, this day of your wedding, is the oc-casion of the
shedding your solitary journeys in favor of bonding yourself with

one another; and your marriage, as well as being the estate of joining with another human being, is also the union of two people committed to the process of their own becoming.

Since you have always attended to your individual selves, to the process of understanding yourselves, healing your own emotional wounds, and learning to be faithful to your prodigious talents, marriage is more than a merging, a blending, or the melting together of the two of you. Rather, it is the ascension of two stately trees growing tall side by side in the forest; it is two angels recognizing one another at the edge of the abyss.

For you marriage is neither absorption nor displacement. Neither of you hopes for, nor would you tolerate, your own disappearance. To be "lost in love" is not your desire; to be subsumed by attachment to someone else's identity is not your image of yourself; to be somebody's "better"—or lesser—half is unthinkable. What you desire and what you require from marriage is somehow different than what is conjured by the usual picture of character-homogenizing wedded bliss. You desire above all the marriage of your true selves; you insist that your marriage be an environment in which as individual beings you can flourish.

Because you believe this so sincerely, because union with individual freedom is what you hope for and intend, there are a number of things to which, as you step across the drawbridge to the castle of marriage, you need to hold fast.

First, remember to honor your individual selves, to keep hold of the vision of your own destinies. This is what you have labored to create; your selves are your greatest treasure, what, in fact, you are each here to share with one another. But while in the past you were able to remember and focus on your journey in a solitary context, now you must be yourself in conjunction with another, and keeping track of your destiny in the midst of a marriage is quite another matter. It's harder; the thrills and demands of the union will distract and charm you and perhaps entice you off your path. But no matter how beautiful or captivating your marriage may be, your relationship as itself can never stand in the place of, nor do service for, what you as individuals came here to accomplish.

In this sense, marriage is the handmaiden of the individuals in it, the supportive context that nourishes the possibilities alive within you. The challenge in marriage is to continue to expand and grow, to honor the full stature of one another, to support the impending expansion that lies within you. Thus, even when you are tempted to dwindle down to the most minimal definition of what being married can be, seeing yourselves only—or first and foremost—as a couple, resist that temptation. Remember that your relationship is a source, the fountain of nourishment for who you both are individually.

Second, remember that your relationship, as itself, has a destiny, and that your marriage is a living, striving organism. It has a nature and attributes of its own that are distinct from, and larger and more intricate than, the characteristics of the individuals it comprises.

One of the oldest human needs is having someone to wonder where you are when you don't come home at night.
—*Margaret Mead*

A relationship has its own mysterious sense of balance, its own timing, its unique choreography, its particular destination. It will carry you along with it to where it needs to go, but if you are overly focused on the *me* and the *I* of yourselves, the relationship itself, that mysterious magical animal, may become starved and lie down like a tired old dog at the side of the road.

So be kind to your relationship. Treat it with respect and nourish it with the entertainments, diversions, purposes, mementos, and happy anticipations it needs to keep it young and puppylike.

And, finally, while you are sailing your little boat on the great sea of marriage, take care as you navigate to avoid being dashed up on either the Sylla of ignoring yourselves or the Charybdis of ignoring the relationship itself; remember to remember love.

For it is love, after all and before all, that has brought you to this place. Love is the inspiration, the magic, and the healing balm of any marriage, no matter how clearly envisioned or powerfully determined its destiny may be. Love is what brought you together; love is what will keep you whole. And so, as you tend to the endless and spirit-unraveling requirements of what your individual destinies will inevitably demand, return in your hearts again and again to the love between you. Love will delight you. Love will most happily distract you when you are tempted to become too serious, too heavy-handed, or overly involved in your own important undertakings. Love will give you joy. Love will give meaning to the pursuit of your destinies. For love is life's highest destiny, its greatest purpose, and its finest work.

✤ THE CONSECRATION ✤

Seeing that no moment is without meaning, no undertaking is without significance, no individual is of such quality as to be diminished by even so important an enterprise as marriage, we ask that you both, together and as your irreplaceably special selves, be honored and expanded by the promises you are about to make, the marriage you are about to create. And may love, that destiny above all destinies, be always in your midst, the handmaid and the master of your marriage.

✤ THE EXPRESSION OF INTENT ✤

Having been reminded once again of the deep value of your own self-knowledge, and understanding that marriage is the convergence of your individual and joint destinies as well as the greatest support for them, that as well as being a mirror for the study of yourselves, your marriage is in itself a worthy enterprise, do you, ____, choose to marry ____, to speak the words that will bind you to her (him) as her husband (his wife) and allow you to become most fully yourself in her (his) presence for the rest of the days of your life?

Answer: I do.

❧ THE VOWS ❧

Dearest ____,
I do now choose you and take you
to be my wife (husband/partner/mate),
to witness and assist in my becoming,
to hold me, as your beloved, in your heart.

I give you my love, the steadfastness
of my purpose, my will, and my hope, and my highest
intention that always, in one another's presence,
we may unflinchingly become who we are, and with
unswerving commitment be willing
to do what we came here to do.

You are my lover, my teacher, my model,
my accomplice, and my true counterpart.
I will love you, hold you, and honor you,
respect you, encourage you, and cherish you,
in health and in sickness
through sorrow and success
for all the days of my life.

❧ THE BLESSING OF THE RINGS ❧

Rings are made precious by our wearing them. They carry our meaning; they say who we are, where we have been, and where we are going. They become us; they reflect us; they are a symbol of our truest essence.

Your wedding rings are most special because they say that even in your uniqueness you have chosen to be bonded, to allow the presence of another human being to enhance who you are. Your rings carry the potent double message: We are individuals and yet we belong; we are not alone. As you wear them through time, they will reflect not only who you are but also the union you are making, the fact that through the rest of your lives each of you will be imprinted by the other, yet as yourself remain.

❧ THE EXCHANGING OF THE RINGS ❧

As a sign of my love
and that I am choosing
to share my whole life's journey
with you, and of my knowing that in marrying
you I shall become much more than I am,
I give you this ring, with the pledge
that with you, I shall become most truly myself
and offer such gifts as I have
and I am to the world.

❧ THE PRONOUNCEMENT OF MARRIAGE ❧

Now having freely chosen to leave behind the private vigil of seeking self-knowledge in solitude, and having taken up the task of clearly seeing and supporting another human being, having promised your love by honoring one another with the gift of your rings, I now pronounce you husband and wife (married).

❧ THE KISS ❧

❧ THE BENEDICTION ❧

May all that you have already become, which has brought you to this day, and all you will become as a consequence of it, in the life-long joining of your hearts and minds continue to show you your purpose.

May you always be brought most beautifully and steadfastly into the presence of yourselves and of one another, and may you live long and happily fulfilling all that you are. Amen.

THE MARRIAGE OF LOVE
AND REJOICING

THE MOOD OF THIS WEDDING IS ONE OF FESTIVITY and well-being. You are here to celebrate your wonderful good fortune and the inevitability of it all, how wonderful it is that you two got together and how deliciously right it feels to love one another. In this ceremony the point is not so much to emphasize the challenges of marriage as to delight in the pure miraculousness that any two people could so happily find and so joyfully come home to one another.

Love really is something over which we have no control. We can need it, wish for it, long for it; but all on our own, even with rigid self-discipline, we cannot insist it into being. Therefore, when love finds us, when the person we simply can't live without crosses our path, it is truly a gift, and the wedding that celebrates this star-fated mating is indeed a happy occasion.

❧ THE CONVOCATION ❧

Love is a miraculous gift, and a wedding is a celebration of that magic, and that's what we're here to do today. We are gathered together to be overjoyed for and with ____ and ____, who are so wonderfully suited to one another that it's a pure delight for the rest of us to see how ebulliently happy two people can be.

When we think of love we sometimes talk about people who "deserve" one another. Not only do ____ and ____ deserve one another, but they are a perfect match, a pair, a fit, two hybrid peas in a pod; and their marriage, far from being something they have had to work hard to achieve, was pure inevitability. They were given to one another and fell so deeply in love that they had no choice.

They are the embodiment of true romance which, matured, becomes true love. They are the example of love that in its light-heartedness dissolves the notion of love as hard work. They are the promise of possibility, the expectation of joyful surprise.

So, hooray! We're here to celebrate, to honor, to laugh, to dance, and to be glad because the inevitable has happened. Love is alive and well in the land. ____ and ____ are here to prove it, and we are here to celebrate with them.

❧ THE INVOCATION ❧

Angels, magicians, wizards, and all good beings, join with us on this happy day and let this be a day of gladness, thanksgiving, possibility, and great good fortune for all of us, but especially for ____ and ____, who are coming together to demonstrate the wonder of love through the celebration of their marriage.

We all live in the hope of loving and being loved, and any sign of the blossoming of love is a true inspiration. Therefore we give thanks for the sweet happiness of ____ and ____. Their enthusiasm is electric, their belief in the destiny of their love is inspiring; their great expectations encourage us beyond measure.

Marriage is a very special place, the sheltered environment in which we can endlessly explore ourselves in the presence of another and in which we can offer the possibility of the true reflection of another. We are so happy that ____ and ____ have found one another, that they know in their souls how perfectly mated they are, and that they are choosing on this day of most special days to become for all time the accurate and beautiful reflection of each other's essence. We ask that the vision they have of one another be always informed by the spellbinding radiant power that first brought them together, and we pray that as they move into the hallowed ground that is marriage they may always hold one another in the light of all light, the love of all love.

❧ THE READINGS ❧

we are so both and oneful (*last stanza*)

we are so both and oneful
night cannot be so sky
sky cannot be so sunful
i am through you so I

—*e. e. cummings*

The Passionate Shepherd to His Love

Come live with me and be my love,
And we will all the pleasures prove
That valleys, groves, hills, and fields,
Woods, or steepy mountain yields.
And we will sit upon the rocks,
Seeing the shepherds feed their flocks,
By shallow rivers to whose falls
Melodious birds sing madrigals.

And I will make thee beds of roses
And a thousand fragrant posies,
A cap of flowers, and a kirtle
Embroidered all with leaves of myrtle;

A gown made of the finest wool
Which from our pretty lambs we pull;
Fair lined slippers for the cold,
With buckles of the purest gold;

A belt of straw and ivy buds,
With coral clasps and amber studs:
And if these pleasures may thee move,
Come live with me, and be my love.
The shepherds' swains shall dance and sing

For thy delight each May morning:
If these delights thy mind may move,
Then live with me and be my love.
—*Christopher Marlowe*

From Sonnets from the Portuguese
How do I love thee? Let me count the ways.
I love thee to the depth and breadth and height
My soul can reach, when feeling out of sight
For the ends of Being and ideal Grace.
I love thee to the level of everyday's
Most quiet need, by sun and candle-light.
I love thee freely, as men strive for Right;
I love thee purely, as they turn from Praise.
I love thee with the passion put to use
In my old griefs, and with my childhood's faith.
I love thee with a love I seemed to lose
With my lost saints—I love thee with the breath,
Smiles, tears, of all my life!—and, if God choose,
I shall but love thee better after death.
—*Elizabeth Barrett Browning*

❧ THE ADDRESS ❧

We're gathered here today to celebrate the wedding of ____ and ____, and we are exuberant and grateful. We're exuberant because, frankly, it's wonderful that ____ and ____ have fallen in love, that they feel so good about one another, so delighted, and encouraged, so known and supported, that they've chosen to risk to love for life, to take the great emotional trapeze leap of linking up with one another in midair and midflight. Their optimism is an inspiration; their daring is exhilarating.

For them, of course, today is absolutely wonderful, a magical rabbit pulled out of life's hat. Out of the routine of ordinary life the extraordinary has happened. They had no idea that they would stumble on one another at (include here a bit of where and how you met: the parking garage where she locked her keys in the car, the train station in Venice, his boss's birthday party . . .), go through all the thrills and frettings of the initial delicious stages of romance, to discover the love of substance and depth they are consecrating with marriage today. They were so happy that they didn't even realize they were serious, that the love that so utterly captivated them, that made them feel like schoolchildren, was also a love of depth and importance. Romance is play, but true love is intention, and it is their intending to love for life that we are celebrating today.

But today is also a celebration for the rest of us, for it is also a pleasure for us to see love in bloom, to participate in the wedding of two people so delightfully suited to one another. It lifts our spirits to be in the presence of such a love, to bask in the sweet energies of two people who so obviously adore one another, who want to play together, laugh together, walk together for a lifetime. Love untarnished, that is the gift that _____ and _____ give us; love with garlands of ribbons and posies, love with infinite hope.

Therefore, _____ and _____, we thank you. You've brightened our day. Thanks for letting us celebrate with you; thanks for showing us that love can bloom, that marriage is a worthy enterprise, and that happy, high-spirited people are overjoyed to undertake it.

And now, before we get to the party, let me say a few words of encouragement and direction to you two. First of all, a wedding is a happy occasion, flawless in its good humor, its joyful sense of well-being, but your marriage won't always be like this. For, as you live it out, you will discover that your relationship has moods and seasons, high times as well as lulls and dead-dog bone-dry gulches. From time to time, the delightful spirit of this wedding day will not be with

Oh, the comfort, the inexpressible comfort of feeling safe with a person, having neither to weigh thoughts nor measure words, but pouring them all right out, just as they are, chaff and grain together; certain that a faithful hand will take and sift them, keep what is worth keeping, and then with the breath of kindness blow the rest away.
—*Dinah Maria Mulock Craik*

you, and when it is taken over by the love grinches, you will have to reach for something deeper in yourselves, for the love that is stronger than feel-good; the love that is truer than fun, the love that requires energy as well as feasts on it.

Your wedding is an unmitigatedly happy occasion, but your marriage will be a many-textured thing. In it, both magic and sorrows will befall you. You will intend one thing and end up doing another. You will imagine your darling to be a certain way and discover that he is not, that she is a person unto herself. You will have clashes and discover things you did and did not want to know. You will rumple each other's spirits as well as bedclothes and hair. You will say mean and terrible words, and, for love, be able to forget them. You will betray one another in tiny and sometimes huge and perhaps devastating ways, and, for love, forgive one another and go on.

Whoever loves true life, will love true love.
—Elizabeth Barrett Browning

These, the great and petty perils of marriage, are an invitation to refine your love and deepen it, to expand it beyond the light-spiritedness and laughter that enliven your hearts today and explore the more profound reaches of compassion, of tender caring, of selfless nurturing. These capacities are the maturing of love through time, love's highest calling and its finest work. And marriage is the summons to be open not only to these challenges but also to the opportunities, unexpected and not necessarily always welcome, that invite them into being.

Second, remember that a relationship is a progression. There's an old Chinese proverb that says: The journey of a thousand miles begins with a single step. For you, _____ and _____, your wedding today is a exquisite and beautifully choreographed first step. With it you are passing through a portal that will lead you to many places, including ones you can't possibly imagine. Wherever it takes you, there will be surprises, for this is the mark of a truly loving relationship—that it will take you where you had not meant to go.

There is great joy to be found in such a surprising journey, with twists and turns, shades and possibilities beyond your wildest imaginings. Instead of resisting the changes, allow them to flower in you and know that they are leading you somewhere, that, separately and together, you are becoming more than you were. Don't expect every day to have the fanciful mood or the exuberant high spirits of this, your wedding day, but be excited, open-minded, curious, available, and inquiring about who you are becoming. Know that your composite experiences are turning you into the highest form of yourselves, that you are becoming the best and the most, that you are doing the things that only you two together could possibly do.

Therefore, along with celebrating the marvelous feelings of today, remember, especially when you are saying your vows, that you are also promising to love for the long and ambiguous future. If you can hold on to this intention, then instead of bowing down or bowing out when you've misplaced your delight, you can ride out the storms with confidence, knowing that the thunderhead-clouded skies are temporary and not a reflection of your relationship as a whole.

Above all, remember that love is what matters. Love will prevail. It is the love you feel for one another that will be the answer to all your difficulties. If in marrying you have chosen well and promised wisely, love will be stronger than the conflicts, bigger than the changes. Love will be the miracle always inviting you to learn, to blossom, to expand. And it is to love—to the love you are celebrating, embodying, and radiating on this special day—that you must always return.

So remember these things, my dear ones, as you go out into the world as a couple: that your love will have seasons, that your relationship is a progression, and that love will prevail. Remembering them, holding them in your hearts and in your minds, will give you a marriage as deep in its joy as your courtship has been in its magic.

Congratulations, ____ and ____, the real fun has just begun.

❧ THE CONSECRATION ❧

Enfolded in joy, inhabited by hope, bathed in the infinite spectrum of light that is love, may you be always infused with it and beautifully illumined by it.

May every desire you have for your love be fulfilled, and may you be given the vision with which to clearly behold one another, the listening with which to perceive one another most genuinely, and the endless generosity of spirit with which to nourish one another's soul and sweetly keep the promises you make here today.

❧ THE EXPRESSION OF INTENT ❧

____ and ____, now that you have heard about the magic and the mysteries of marriage, the way it will continually surprise you, the strength and wisdom it will everlastingly ask of you, do you choose still and happily and in our midst to make the promises of marriage?

Do you ____ want to marry ____, to happily hold her (him) above all and have her (him) as your bride and wife (groom and husband, life partner)?

Answer: I certainly do.

❧ THE VOWS ❧

From this day on I choose you, my beloved ____,
to be my wife (husband/mate/life partner),
to live with you and laugh with you;
to stand by your side and sleep in your arms;
to be joy to your heart and food to your soul;
to bring out the best in you always;
and, for you, to be the most that I can.

To laugh with you in the good times;
to struggle with you in the bad;
to solace you when you are downhearted;
to wipe your tears with my hands;
to comfort you with my body;
to mirror you with my soul;
to share with you all my riches and honors;

to play with you as much as I can
until we grow old, and still loving
each other sweetly and gladly,
our lives shall come to the end.

❧ THE BLESSING OF THE RINGS ❧

These rings are made of precious metals, a symbol of the riches that
reside in each of you; and as any metal is purified by the white heat
of testing, so will your love be purified by the tests facing you through
the many seasons of your life.

    These rings are made with precious jewels; and as the elements
from which these jewels are formed are ancient as the stars, as mysterious as moonlight, and as shining as the miracle of your
new-bonded radiance, wear them as the sign of the love ignited
between you, the love unquenchable which now your hearts embody
and your words express.

❧ THE EXCHANGING OF THE RINGS ❧

Dearest, ____, my love,
this ring is the token of my love
and of the hopes and all the joys
I most dearly behold in you.

You are my promise and my
most magically answered plea,
you are my wish, my dream, my quest;
you are my gift, my lover, my double,
my perfectly matching mate.

You are my light, my love, my limbs,
my soul's most mirroring shadow,
my body's closest friend.

I marry you with this ring,
with the wings of my love,
with all that I have and I am.

Answer:
Thank you, my love.
I will wear forever this ring
as the sign of my joy
and the depth of your love.

❧ THE PRONOUNCEMENT OF MARRIAGE ❧

____ and ____, now that you have heard the words about love and marriage, now that you have shown us the example of your love and celebrated your union by giving each other these beautiful rings, it is with great joy and happiness that I now pronounce you husband and wife (married). You may now kiss.

❧ THE KISS ❧

❧ THE BENEDICTION ❧

God bless you, beautiful young ones. May the wings of angels uphold you through all the life of your love; may you live forever in happiness with one another. May your hearts be full; may your lips stay sweet. May your love grow strong; may you love long and happily in one another's arms.

THE MARRIAGE OF LOVE
AND FULFILLMENT

✍

IF YOU HAVE BEEN MARRIED BEFORE, YOU ARE NO doubt approaching this new marriage with feelings that differ markedly from those you had when you were a first-time bride or groom. Subsequent marriages represent commitment in the face of disappointment or loss; celebration tempered by a previous experience of disillusionment. Therefore, in both what you say to one another and what you choose to have said at your ceremony, you will want to acknowledge that as well as celebrating the love you share now, you are remembering the love that wounded you in the past.

Sometimes this wounding was betrayal, a trust that was broken; sometimes it was the unbearable sorrow of losing a mate to death. As this ceremony is geared to those previously divorced, if you are a widow or widower marrying again, you may want to tailor this ceremony a little more precisely to your needs.

When it comes to losses—in life and in love—we all tend to want to let bygones be bygones, to shove our mistakes and disheartenments under the rug. Of course it's nice, if you can, to put your troubles out of your mind. But if you want this marriage to be a success, and if you want this wedding to catapult you into the relationship that really will last the rest of your life, don't try to bury the truth about your past. Instead, let the uniqueness of this wedding celebration arise precisely from the fact that it stands in counterpoint to a marriage or marriages which, for one reason or another, came to an end. Be bold in celebrating your hopes and in enlisting the support of your friends, as you have the courage, once again—and differently—to make your marriage vows.

❧ THE CONVOCATION ❧

We have come here together today to celebrate the marriage and reflect the incredible joy of ____ and ____, who, after several dress rehearsals and detours (or after almost overwhelming losses), long after they believed that it was possible, have been given the great good fortune of falling in love with one another.

A wedding is the celebration of the miracle of love, and that's what we're here to do: to celebrate that miracles do occur; that at any moment, the unexpected can happen; and that after almost giving up hope, most inexplicably and wonderfully, the path of our entire lives can change.

Marriage is a meditation on our histories as well as on our future, on our losses and failures, as well as our hopes and possibilities. And so, as ____ and ____ wed, it is worthwhile to contemplate that they could not and would not be standing before us today if they had not followed their own star home and done what they needed to do to deliver themselves to this point in their lives.

____ and ____, you give us hope, and we are overjoyed to be your witnesses. You are the living embodiment of the truth that practice does indeed make perfect, that persistence does, in fact, pay off. We are touched by your happiness; we are moved by the exquisite courage of your love. It gives us incomparable joy to celebrate with you, to be reminded that true love, abiding love, is the consequence of the practice of love, and that nothing we do in this life is ever wasted or lost.

❧ THE INVOCATION ❧

God, the great magician, you leave us spellbound with your generosity. In bringing ____ and ____ together, you invite us to comprehend that love is a profound and mysterious process, and that because of—and in spite of—those with whom we have shared our lives in the past, we have been ineluctably shaped as ourselves.

In delivering _____ and _____ to this place, you teach us to comprehend that love is a process. It is the unfolding, honing, grinding, and preparing of ourselves that enables us to stand in the presence of another human being and embrace that person with the love we have been waiting a lifetime to experience.

We thank you for this miraculous day, for the fulfillment of love we see before us, and for the joy of sharing this happy occasion.

❧ THE READINGS ❧

The Ivy Crown
The whole process is a lie,
    unless,
        crowned by excess,
it break forcefully,
    one way or another,
        from its confinement—
or find a deeper well.
    Anthony and Cleopatra
        were right;
they have shown
    the way. I love you
        or I do not live
at all.
Daffodil time
    is past. This is
        summer, summer!
the heart says,
    and not even the full of it.
        No doubts
are permitted—
    though they will come
        and may
before our time

    overwhelm us.
        We are only mortal
but being mortal
    can defy our fate.
        We may
by an outside chance
    even win! We do not
        look to see
jonquils and violets
    come again
        but there are,
still,
    the roses!

Romance has no part in it.
    The business of love is
        cruelty which,
by our wills,
    we transform
        to live together.
It has its seasons,
    for and against,
        whatever the heart
fumbles in the dark
    to assert
        toward the end of May.
Just as the nature of briars
    is to tear flesh,
        I have proceeded
through them.
    Keep
        the briars out,
they say.
    You cannot live

    and keep free of
briars.

Children pick flowers.
    Let them.
       Though having them
in hand
    they have no further use for them
       but leave them crumpled
at the curb's edge.

At our age the imagination
    across the sorry facts
       lifts us
to make roses
    stand before thorns.
       Sure
love is cruel
    and selfish
       and totally obtuse—
at least, blinded by the light,
    young love is.
       But we are older,
I to love
    and you to be loved,
       we have,
no matter how,
    by our wills survived
       to keep
the jeweled prize
    always
       at our finger tips.
We will it so
    and so it is
       past all accident.
            —*William Carlos Williams*

❧ THE ADDRESS ❧

Marriage is a bonding of strangers made beautifully familiar through the miracle of love, the process of unstrangering one another through the power of loving and the gift of time. Marriage brings two people together not only in the present, but in the presence of their past— of the lives they have led, the choices they have made, the lessons that have shaped and reshaped the chambers of their hearts. Thus to be marrying again is different than simply to be marrying.

And so, as you contemplate reentering the very state that wounded you, you may be tempted to blind yourself to all the sorrows, difficulties, and disappointments of your past relationships, to look at this marriage as separate, distinct, and completely unrelated to all the relationships that preceded it.

This is a worthy temptation; it would be wonderful to think that this relationship—and your readiness for it—arrived at your doorstep out of the blue. But that isn't the case, and in trying to view it this way you separate yourself from the lessons that brought you here, indeed from your own evolution as a person. For the other relationships you've had, you went through not *instead of* being in this relationship, but *in order* to be in it. This marriage is the culmination of years of apprenticeship, the winnowing and honing of your previous relationships to help shape you into the person who stands here today, ready to make the ultimate commitment of love.

Therefore, when you doubt the relevance of your past—and you will at times—or when you feel embarrassed about it—which, at times, you may—remember that every relationship you have had was a step on the path to this one. The past was a prologue. Every single conflict and disappointment, every beautiful, grueling, and painfully instructive moment in each of those relationships was delivered to your consciousness in preparation for this love.

Your experiences then are the laundry ticket for the silk garments you are retrieving from the cleaners now. What you did then was the antecedent, the exquisitely appropriate conditioning for what you are doing now. Everything was of value; everything taught you something, prepared you for marrying again, most happily now.

Acknowledging the past as preparation allows you to step most gracefully into the present, and, having done so, you need to remind each other that this union is unique. This is not just "another relationship"; it is the consequence and fulfillment of all those that have gone before. It is the last and the best. It has qualities contributed by both of you that make it the highest expression of what you two can offer through the medium of an intimate relationship. Therefore, be generous in reminding one another not only of what a gem of a relationship you have here, but also of the singular set of qualities you each possess—the attributes, values, and convictions—that can allow you to legitimately believe to the depths of your hearts that this is the love that will last until the end of your days.

Sometimes when we've finally arrived at a longed-for destination, there's a temptation simply to be where we are, without discovering the possibilities inherent to our new state. This marriage may feel like a destination, a sweet safe place in which you can finally rest; but it is also an opportunity, the emotional and spiritual environment in which you can both develop to your highest brilliance. This is the person with whom you can do all the precious things you've wanted all your life to do. This is the time to receive and intend, to fulfill not only the joy of your heart but the possibilities of your life.

Therefore, remember to do the simple and beautiful things that will make this love a treasure. Play. Fight well. Communicate with one another. Focus on what you want, and entice your intentions into being. Plan for the things that are important to you, and make sure you do them. This love is to be nurtured, to be lived out to the fullest in every aspect of its dreams—in the simple ceremonies of shared daily life, in realized hopes and long-deferred plans, in a quality of emotional exchange and spiritual communion toward which the whole of your life has been leaning.

> To live without loving is not really to live.
> —*Moliere*

And, finally, be thankful for one another. Love is always a gift. A great compliment is being paid to you in being given another chance, another opportunity to love. You have been delivered to your ultimate partner, the person with whom you can share the fruits of all the lessons in your life. Not everyone has this opportunity; not everyone is granted this cornucopia of happiness.

This love was completely unexpected, the joyful consequence of nothing you could control. Although everything you have experienced prepared you for it, there was nothing you could do to actually bring it into being; and so it is, indeed, one of life's miracles.

In the presence of a miracle, one of the great human impulses is to disbelieve it or think that somehow we are not worthy of it. Yet it is in the very nature of miracles that we are unworthy of them, that we ourselves did nothing to bring them about. The way to be worthy of the miracle of this love is, simply, to receive it; open your heart, your hands, your eyes, and allow the radiance of this love, this love for which you have waited so long, for which you have learned so much, to utterly and endlessly illuminate you.

Love is the gift that has been given to you, and it is also the gift that you must now give back: to embody, to live out the love, the hope, the joy, the incomparable radiance, and the incredible mirroring that you have had the great good fortune to be given.

❧ THE CONSECRATION ❧

Now that you, ____ and ____, have heard about the path of relationship and can rest in the expectation that the love you have found is the fulfillment of the loves you have lost, we ask that your hearts remain always open with thanksgiving for the miracle that has befallen you, for such happiness ofttimes does not occur. Also, may the promises you make to one another be lived out to the end of your days in an atmosphere of the profoundest joy.

❧ THE EXPRESSION OF INTENT ❧

____, knowing that your heart has been bruised, that the path of marriage has not always brought you joy, that because of your sorrows you have doubted your wisdom and the wholeness of the self that did the choosing, do you choose now, with fresh joy and new love, to marry ____ for the long unfurling future, and for the ever-remaining seasons of your life?

Answer: I do.

❧ THE VOWS ❧

____, my beloved,
emptying my heart of all others,
I fill it now with you,
to love you until the end of my days
as my most treasured wife (husband/spouse/mate).

Remembering the sorrows that have brought me
to this place, acknowledging the lessons I have learned,
I set them all aside, and make my life with you.

I will love you, hold you, and honor you
in good times and in bad,
enjoy you, console you, delight you,
astound you when I can,
give thanks for you always,
and cherish you dearly
until the end of our days.

❧ THE BLESSING OF THE RINGS ❧

Rings are objects of adornment, and while, in a single lifetime, we may have many objects of adornment, we have among them always the one that is most precious to us. May these rings, from this day forward, be your most treasured adornment; and may the love they symbolize be, to the end of your days, your most precious possession.

❧ THE EXCHANGING OF THE RINGS ❧

This ring is my thanksgiving,
my promise that I will always love you,
that I will always cherish you
and honor you
for all the days of my life.

❧ THE PRONOUNCEMENT OF MARRIAGE ❧

With the sense of incomparable joy that you have found emotional sanctuary for your heart, that you have discovered your life's true love, I now pronounce you husband and wife (married). You may now seal your marriage with a kiss.

❧ THE KISS ❧

❧ THE BENEDICTION ❧

May you live out your days in joy, may you live in one another's company in peace, and may your days be filled with the rewards of all you have endured to bring you to this place. May you endlessly delight one another and may you love and fulfill each other always.

THE MARRIAGE OF LOVE
AND RENEWAL

ANY MARRIAGE IS A WONDERFUL OCCASION, THE formal expression of love for two people who are solemnizing their bonds of affection with marriage vows. But for persons recovering from an addiction of any kind, marriage is often the highest reward of having finally come to love themselves in a way that for so long they believed impossible.

As anyone who has undergone or is undergoing the process of healing from an addiction will know, a relationship is one of the things you must set aside in order to accomplish your own healing. In this sense, in the initial stages of recovery, solitude is one of the prices you pay for the possibility of redeeming and renewing your life. Later on, however, a relationship becomes the fulfillment of what you have undertaken in the bravery of solitude, the happy consequence of the painstaking process of personal healing.

Because your recovery is the other most important thing in your life and because you have deep feelings about it, you may want your wedding to be an occasion for opening your heart to your sense of gratitude for the new life given you through your recovery process. The point of view of The Marriage of Love and Renewal is that, rather than holding this truth in abeyance, treating it like a shameful secret you want kept to yourself or hidden between the lines, you are choosing not only to reveal it but to have your recovery itself be acknowledged as a reason for celebration. Not only are you getting married, you are overjoyed that you are no longer walking through life with the albatross of addiction hanging around your neck. Rather than keep this truth in the background, you want to bring it forward, making it if not the primary focus, then at least certainly a matter worthy of mention in the course of your wedding ceremony.

I would strongly encourage you to do this. All too often we treat the sorrows, losses, and difficulties that have shaped our lives like ugly stepchildren who should be kept out of sight, sweeping up the ashes at the hearth. In truth, it is in our transcendence of them that we become most truly ourselves, and in openly acknowledging them we not only gain a sense of our power over them but also discover a great measure of thanksgiving for the miracle of our survival.

No occasion could be more perfect to acknowledge such beautiful victories than a wedding. So if you are a person who carries one of these spiritual achievements in your bag of tricks, you may want to consider the following ceremony as the appropriate vehicle for expressing your most precious feelings about the life you have left and the new life that awaits you in marriage. Let this be an opportunity to acknowledge, not only to your beloved but to all the people celebrating with you, that indeed you have rejoined the living and that your marriage represents the highest reward of your personal transformation.

❧ THE CONVOCATION ❧

We have come together with great happiness to acknowledge the new life and the emotional delight of ____ and ____, who after struggling with enemies without and within have become the happy and grateful participants in a deep and abiding love.

A wedding is always a happy occasion, but this one is all the more joyful because it represents not only the coming together of two wonderful people but also the fulfillment of the liberation of their individual selves, the completion of a healing that required great faith and took thousands of intricate steps to accomplish. This is a process with which we can all identify. For although we generally think of recovery as a release from the abuse of a specific substance, all of us struggle against our own personal odds to become most fully ourselves.

We are happy for ____ and ____ and grateful to them because

they embody the miracle of the possible. They stand before us revealing the power of love to heal. They teach us that loving yourself is a worthy enterprise. They show us that self-love creates the window of possibility of love between one another.

Their ability to transform their difficulties into new and shining possibilities bodes well for their marriage. For transformation is an unavoidable consequence of marriage, in a sense its greatest achievement; and so as they enter into marriage and even more as they live their lives inside its hallowed gates, rather than resisting the transformations that are the hallmark of love's work, they are already well equipped to embrace the process that will constantly reshape them. They have already shown their willingness to grow beyond their limitations, and we join them gladly in the formal solemnizing of their willingness to continue this beautiful process through their marriage.

❧ INVOCATION ❧

We stand on tiptoe with thanksgiving for the love that has united _____ and _____, the visible reward of their healing and the consecration of their individual lives. We ask that this day be a true celebration not only for them but also for us. Allow us to be inspired by the example of their healing, enlarged by their joy, and delighted by the happiness they have brought into our midst. We give thanks for this beautiful day, for this marvelous occasion, and for the love which is the bond that binds them each to one another and to all of us.

❧ THE READINGS ❧

Ecclesiastes 4:9–12

Two are better than one, because they have a good reward for their toil. For if they fall, one will lift up his fellow; but woe to him who is alone when he falls and has not another to lift him up. Again, if two lie together, they are warm; but how can one be warm alone? And though a man might prevail against one who is alone, two will withstand him.

Colossians 3:12–14
As therefore, God's picked representatives of the new humanity, purified and beloved of God himself, be merciful in action, kindly in heart, humble in mind. Accept life, and be most patient and tolerant with one another, always ready to forgive if you have a difference with anyone. Forgive as freely as the Lord has forgiven you. And, above all, be truly loving, for love is the golden chain of all the virtues.

To Althea, from Prison (*last stanza*)
Stone walls do not a prison make,
Nor iron bars a cage;
Minds innocent and quiet take
That for an hermitage.
If I have freedom in my love,
And in my soul am free,
Angels alone, that soar above,
Enjoy such liberty.
                        —*Richard Lovelace*

somewhere i have never travelled
somewhere i have never travelled, gladly beyond
any experience, your eyes have their silence:
in your most frail gesture are things which enclose me,
or which i cannot touch because they are too near

your slightest look easily will unclose me
though i have closed myself as fingers,
you open always petal by petal myself as Spring opens
(touching skillfully, mysteriously) her first rose

or if your wish be to close me, i and
my life will shut very beautifully, suddenly,
as when the heart of this flower imagines
the snow carefully everywhere descending;

nothing which we are to perceive in this world equals
the power of your intense fragility: whose texture
compels me with the colour of its countries,
rendering death and forever with each breathing

(i do not know what it is about you that closes
and opens; only something in me understands
the voice of your eyes is deeper than all roses)
nobody, not even the rain, has such small hands
                    —*e. e. cummings*

❧ THE ADDRESS ❧

There are prisons of the heart and mind, cages in which we lock up
our emotions and incarcerate our spirits, which limit our possibilities and are more devastatingly disruptive to our lives than any
concrete limitations that can be imposed upon us from the outside.
Habits, practices, and substances through which we disown ourselves are among the worst dungeons we can create, and the climb
back to light from such darknesses requires that we walk through
the pain of all we have tried to erase through anaesthetizing ourselves. That journey is a most demanding and heroic one, one that
makes walking down the aisle look like a hop, skip, and a jump
through a daisy-dappled meadow.

   It may seem odd to mention the recovery from an addiction at a
wedding, but to ____ and/(or) ____, the deliverance from this bondage
was the most important undertaking of her (and/or his) life, a movement from the darkness of annihilation to the bright day of new life,
and it is from this happy ground that their love springs.

Love is the ultimate result of any process of self-healing; and marriage, living in the presence of another human being as your whole and liberated self, is one of its happiest consequences. Because of your hard work and steadfast commitment, you have each been given one of life's greatest gifts—the opportunity to live in the presence of another human being while discovering your own capacity to bloom.

Just as the recovery from an addiction seeks no reward but itself, so marriage seeks no reward but itself: the simple ineffable joys of living the days of your life with a person who has been given to cherish you.

Therefore, on this happy occasion let us consider certain things. First of all, as you enter into your marriage, remember where you came from. By this I mean that as you proceed on your way, on the emotional merry-go-round of marriage with its unsettlements that can discombobulate you and delights that can equally overwhelm you, remember where you have come from. That is, remember that you weren't always happy and in love. Remember that you were someone who glimpsed the pit of hell in your own particular fashion, and that hell is indeed a real place.

> It is the special quality of love not to be able to remain stationary, to be obliged to increase under pain of diminishing.
> —*Andre Gide*

Remember the look of the sky when you could see it only through the bars of the narrow prison window, when you were shut inside the jail of your own making while life continued on the outside, distant and intangible, unattainable to you. Give proper respect to the fact that you, like most of us, could draw your world so small that you allowed yourself to be separated from love, from the human community, and from the riches in yourself. Remember the small, pinched life you had and the courageous struggle you went through to liberate yourself from it.

Second, after you've remembered who you were and where you've been, forget the monster-infested forests you came from. The very things that are important to remember are also important to forget; and, after taking note of the not-so-happy times in your past, be willing to put them behind you. That's not what your life is about anymore; that's not where you are now. That's not who you are now. Living is. Loving is.

And, finally, after remembering and forgetting where you have been, go where you are heading. Marriage is a new phase, and this, the day of your wedding, is the occasion of your joining forces with someone who loves you, just as you are, with all your flaws and potential, with all that you have been, and with all that you are becoming. She has her own struggles, her own demons to be fought. He has his own wounds and possibilities, his own, in the words of e. e. cummings, "intense fragility." Staying open to your beloved while remaining true to yourself, treating one another's wounds with tenderness, discovering the power of your gifts and your responsibilities for them, expanding your emotional repertoire to include righteous conflict and the nurturing of your spirits—these are your challenges now.

This is the beginning of a beautiful new chapter of your life. This chapter is vibrant and dramatic; it contains dreams and possibilities, forward movement, action, and endless realizable potential. You have graduated from the phase of life that you devoted to overcoming something, and matriculated into the powerful and wonderful adventure of life as it is now. This chapter is a yes, this chapter is a hurray! This is the coming-out party of all coming-out parties—you as yourself loving someone as him(her)self and believing in a future alive with possibilities.

It is the very act of marrying that creates the possibility of this further transformation. For marriage is more than merely making your life with someone. Marriage is a special kind of sanctuary, a spiritual wing of protection; for in choosing to commit to this degree and to make public your choice, to submerge and submit your relationship in the midst of the community, you are inviting yourselves to be true to it, not open-endedly, not merely on a whim or as an experiment, but under the canopy of a lifetime promise. In and through this sanctuary, you make to your beloved a lifelong commitment as sacred as the one you have made to yourself, and the future is transformed by your pledge to go "somewhere i have never travelled gladly beyond any experience."

Therefore, ____ and ____, with our love and congratulations we set you a-sail in the brave little boat of your marriage, urging you both to remember and forget the difficult landscapes that you have traveled through, always recognizing that love is the ultimate recovery, the happiest destination, and the highest of all rewards. We wish you godspeed on your beautiful journey together.

❧ THE CONSECRATION ❧

In the eyes of God, the present is infinitely forever. So let this moment, the apogee of your individual healings, be the present truth that forever eclipses the sorrows of your past. As your lives have opened to the joy of being most wholly and happily yourselves, may you be given the sweetness of heart and the steadfastness of spirit to live in the joy upon joy of loving one another always.

❧ THE EXPRESSION OF INTENT ❧

Therefore, ____, after all you have been through, and after hearing these words about the possibilities and requirements, the rememberings and forgettings of marriage, do you now choose to come home to the sanctuary of marriage and have ____ as your wife (husband/partner/mate)?

Answer: I do.

❧ THE VOWS ❧

Because you have witnessed the healing
of my wounds and solaced me in my sorrow,
you have awakened the joy in my heart

and restored well-being to my spirit.
Surely all this goodness can be no mistake,
and is a promise of the miracles to come.
Therefore, I choose you and take you this day
to become my beloved wife (husband/partner/mate).
One day at a time, I promise to love you,
to hold you in my heart and with my body,
and, in honor of our love, to steadfastly
pursue the life that makes me whole.

I will support you always in the beautiful
and ever-unfolding process of your healing.
I will honor you in all your undertakings
and stand at your side in times of discouragement and testing.
I will care for you in sickness, enjoy you in health,
give thanks for you always, and with a glad heart
I shall treasure you all the days of our lives.

This is my heartfelt promise. This is my solemn vow.

❧ THE BLESSING OF THE RINGS ❧

Wholeness is the state in which nothing is missing and everything is possible, in which what has been is completed by what is, and in which there is no lack. These rings represent wholeness, a coming around of the cycle: from sickness to health, from want to plenty, from despair to joy, from failure to possibility, from loneliness to love.

Let these rings also be a sign that love has substance as well as soul, a present as well as a past, and that, despite its occasional sorrows, love is a circle of happiness, wonder, and delight.

❧ THE EXCHANGING OF THE RINGS ❧

I give you this ring as a token of my abiding love,
as a sign that I have chosen you above all others,
that we shall together go through more than we have
already been through,
and of the hope that the treasures of our future
shall render invisible the sorrows of our past.
I love you.

❧ THE PRONOUNCEMENT OF MARRIAGE ❧

Now, because you have chosen one another, honored each other with
the precious gift of your rings, and pledged to love each other for all
the days of your lives, it gives me great joy to pronounce you husband
and wife (married). You may kiss.

❧ THE KISS ❧

❧ THE BENEDICTION ❧

May the higher power that has given you the gift of healing and the
miracle of this marriage guard your well-being and fill your days
with joy and happiness in the presence of one another. Go in peace;
live in joy. Thanks be to God.

THE CIVIL CEREMONY

THE CIVIL CEREMONY IS THE SIMPLEST, MOST immediate and direct of all the wedding ceremonies. It is usually attended only by the bride, the groom, and the legally required witnesses. It includes a brief form of the convocation, the vows, and the pronouncement. If you would like this shorthand wedding, here is a sample upon which you can base your own.

Officiant: We have come together to unite the two of you in marriage, which is an institution ordained by the state and made honorable by the faithful keeping of good men and women in all ages, and is not to be entered into lightly or unadvisedly.

Then, the officiant turns to the groom and says:
    Do you take _____ to be your wife, to love, honor, comfort, and cherish from this day forth?
    Answer: I do.

Then, turning to the bride:
    Do you take _____ to be your husband, to love, honor, comfort, and cherish from this day forth?
    Answer: I do.
If you are having a ring ceremony, here is where you exchange the rings.

Officiant: Having pledged yourselves each to the other, I do now, by virtue of the authority vested in me by the state of [state], pronounce you husband and wife.

THE QUAKER CEREMONY

THE WEDDING IS HELD DURING A WORSHIP MEETING. The couple enter and take seats at the front of the room. In giving themselves to each other, they eliminate the custom of another person's "giving away" the bride. And because Friends believe that God alone can create a marriage union, no third person announces the couple husband and wife (not having an officiant is legal only in certain states. If you are interested in such a wedding, you need to check on its legality.)

In an atmosphere of quiet and reverence, the couple arises and take one another by the hand. One after another they recite their promise:

"In the presence of God and these our friends, I take thee, ____, to be my wife/husband, and promise, with Divine assistance, to be unto thee a loving and faithful wife/husband so long as we both shall live."

The couple then sit down again and the marriage certificate, which announces the vows they have just taken, is brought for them to sign. Then someone reads the certificate aloud. The meeting continues in silent waiting upon God while those assembled share in the worship through prayer and meditation or through spoken messages. When the meeting is through, those present are asked to sign the certificate as witnesses to the marriage.

ADDITIONAL
SELECTIONS

✣ PROCESSION ✣

The Christian Procession

The traditional procession from the Christian faith is designed in such way as to symbolize what Christ said about marriage: that through it "a man will leave his father and mother and cleave unto his wife, and a woman will leave her father and mother to cleave unto her husband." In the traditional Christian wedding, the procession is a visible, physical enactment of this transition and ordinarily utilizes the following design.

After all the guests have been seated, the groom's mother is escorted to the front row on the right side of the church. This, of course, is ordinarily done by an usher, who will stand at her right, pause with her at the front row, and allow her to take her seat. If you are not having ushers at your wedding but want to follow this tradition, have the groom's father escort the groom's mother, or, if he is deceased or for some other reason not present, have the groom's mother walk down the aisle alone and seat herself in the front row on the right. Otherwise, as she is proceeding to the front of the church, the groom's father, unescorted, will follow close behind her, seating himself at her side in the place closest to the aisle on the right side of the church.

In many ancient traditions, the left side of the body is seen to be the feminine side, the right, the masculine. Thus, in the seating of the bride's and groom's parents and friends in "the body" of witnesses, the groom's parents are located on the right, symbolizing the masculine presence in the marriage, and the bride's on the left, embodying the feminine.

The bride's mother then follows, escorted by an usher, who stands to her right and delivers her to her place in the front row on the left side of the church. Note that the usher stands *to the right* of both the bride's and groom's mother; he should step back slightly as they arrive at the pew so the woman he is escorting may comfortably assume her seat.

The seating of the bride's mother is the traditional indication that the wedding is about to begin. The ushers then unroll the white carpet, if there is to be one. This sets the stage for the next part of the procession.

At this point the officiant enters, usually from a side door or side aisle of the church or gathering place, to take his or her place at the altar or focal point for the ceremony. The officiant's presence presages the arrival of the couple, and brings the preparatory part of the ceremony—the musical prelude and gathering of the guests—to a conclusion.

Once the officiant is situated, the groom, with his best man immediately following, takes his place at the front of the church on the right. He may then immediately turn and face the door of the church from which the bride and her father will presently enter, or he may wait to do this until he receives the cue from the bride's mother.

It should be noted here that in the traditional Christian ceremony it is the bride's mother (the woman whose nurturing and example have been the model for the bride both as a woman and as a wife) who provides the cues for the guests. It is she who stands and turns in anticipation of the bride's arrival, and she who sits down first, once the bride and her father have arrived at the altar, thus indicating to the guests that they should now be seated. Her movement, as all movement in the wedding procession, is beautifully symbolic. As she stands to greet and acknowledge the bride, it's as if she is saying, "I have completed my work; I await and honor the woman I have created through my love and care and example"; then, as she sits down: "I am here to release her, no longer to be active, but a loving passive witness as my daughter enters her new life."

Because the formality of the role of the bride's mother has been frequently departed from in recent years, if you want to follow this tradition, it would be wise to have the ushers tell all the guests that they should stand when the bride's mother stands, turn when she turns, and sit down when she sits down. Or, if you have a guest book at the entrance to the ceremony or are using a written order of service, you may want to specify these directions there.

Following the seating of the mother of the bride, the ushers proceed down the aisle, taking their places alongside the groom and best man. Once they are situated, the bridesmaids begin their procession, and take their places on the left at the front of the church, leaving room for the maid of honor and the bride herself. Following all the bridesmaids, and dressed like them or wearing a gown particular to her, the maid of honor will enter, taking her place to the right of the bridesmaids and leaving a place for the bride at the center of the aisle, directly in front of the altar.

The maid of honor is followed by the ring-bearer, a child, usually a boy, bearing the actual rings or a facsimile of them, usually on a special pillow, then by the flower girl or girls, who scatter the aisle with flowers for the bride to walk on. Once the path for the bride has been thus prepared, the organist or musicians begin playing the traditional wedding march (or whatever piece of music has been selected for the bride's processional entrance).

As you see, we have moved, in true ceremonial fashion, from a general to a more specific focus, from a casual to the more and more intense level of anticipation. By now the groom, groomsmen, bridesmaids, maid of honor, ring bearer, flower girl, and bride's mother should all be standing and facing the central aisle in expectation of the entrance of the bride, who will be on her father's right arm as he escorts her down the aisle. This is the first high moment of the wedding.

The bride is delivered to the altar by her father, who then, traditionally, kisses her farewell. This symbolizes that she has now left home and family, and been given into the authority of the church, which will now initiate her into the sacred estate of matrimony. Her father then takes his place in the pew beside the bride's mother, and the ceremony begins.

True love hurts. It always has to hurt. It must be painful to love someone, painful to leave them, you might have to die for them. When people marry they have to give up everything to love each other. The mother who gives birth to her child suffers much. It is the same for us in the religious life. To belong fully to God we have to give up everything. Only then can we truly love. The word "love" is so misunderstood and so misused.

—*Mother Teresa*

The Jewish Procession

In the Jewish ceremony it is not only the bride but also the groom who is brought to the huppah, or ceremonial canopy, by the parents. The groom walks in first, accompanied his mother and father. Once he is situated, the bride is escorted down the aisle by both her parents.

Once the bride and groom are standing under the huppah with the rabbi, both sets of parents may remain standing behind members of the wedding. If they choose to be seated, however, the groom's parents should sit on the left side of the room, with the groom's guests, the bride's mother and father on the right, with hers. You will note that this placement of both parents and guests is exactly opposite that of the Christian ceremony. At an Orthodox Jewish ceremony, women and men may be asked to sit on separate sides of the room.

❦ CONVOCATION ❦

We are assembled here today because love gathers us, and, especially, because love has found ____ and ____ and woven them together into the great web of life.

We are gathered to remember and rejoice, to recount with one another that it is love, always love, that leads us to our true destination and to celebrate that ____ and ____ have finally arrived.

We have come together also to honor the paradox that the choosing of one is the leaving of all others, the destination is the beginning, that the joy shall bring tears to our eyes.

We are here to celebrate the marriage of ____ and ____, to honor the beginning of their new life.

———— ♆ ————

Come on now, pull up your chairs, open your hearts, turn off your minds. We've come here together to celebrate and have fun, to see what magic and moonlight have done, to see how love can make a king and queen out of a man and woman.

This is a wedding, ____'s and ____'s wedding, and we're here to listen, to love and sing and dance and rejoice, and to send them into their future, with one outrageous, gigantic blessing.

So sit back now, open your hearts, and let the wedding begin.

Come, let us make a circle together and be glad. Let us clap our hands and rejoice. Let us open our mouths and sing a fine song, for the single path has been doubled, the empty hearth has been filled with new fire, and the bride and bridegroom have come.

"How beautiful upon the mountains are the feet of him that brings good tidings, that publishes peace." From time immemorial people have been drawn together in times of sorrow and in times of great joy, to share their burdens, to lift high their exultant cry of celebration. So it is that we, today, have come together to witness and commemorate with a man and woman the creation of their union and for their creation among us of a new home. We gather with them and rejoice; this is a most sacred hour and we are moved to thanksgiving.

—Adapted from a Baptist ceremony

Dearly beloved, we are gathered together here in the sight of God and in the face of this company to join together this man and this woman in holy matrimony; which is an honorable estate, instituted of God, signifying the mystical union between Christ and his church, which holy estate Christ adorned and beautified with his presence and his first miracle at the wedding at Cana of Galilee, and is commended of Saint Paul to be honorable among all men: and therefore is not by any to be entered into unadvisedly or lightly, but reverently, discreetly, advisedly, soberly, and in the fear of God. Into this holy estate these two persons present come now to be joined. If any man can show just cause why they may not lawfully be joined together, let him now speak, or else hereafter hold his peace.

—The Book of Common Prayer

❧ INVOCATION ❧

Divine light that illumines our hearts and gives life to each cell of our being, we give thanks for the love that has gathered us together in this place, and especially for the beautiful, heartwarming love that _____ and _____ have chosen this day to consecrate in marriage.

For all the beauty that you have lodged in them we give great thanks, for their open hearts and loving spirits, for their wisdom in choosing to love, for their willingness to walk on the path of true love, with all its joys and burdens and lessons.

Bless them now with your joyful abundant radiance, so that the words they say, the feelings that beautifully transform them in these moments, and the dreams that they dare to dream can be lived out in their married life as illumination incarnate.

In this sacred and joyful moment we call upon the highest in _____ and _____, the divine inner presence that always knows exactly what you need, that gives and asks the best of you, that brought you to love and has chosen for you the sweet commitment of marriage. For you we ask every blessing of this moment: a confirmation of the wisdom of your choice; great happiness on the path that is set before you; discretion, kindness, and care as you walk upon it; strength to live out your purpose; grace and peace through each step of your journey; and beloved friends to support you.

May you be filled with joy; may you keep your promises with ease; may love abide with you always.

> When we love, we bring out the most beautiful parts of the other person. That's real magic.
>
> *—Jean Shinoda Bolen*

———— ℘ ————

Dear and kind God,

We ask for the bliss of your blessing on ____ and ____, your beautiful children whom you have brought into life in your radiant image.

Be with them, and with us also, in this lovely and sacred moment of their marriage, and bring forth in them all the strength and beauty and love they will need to make every word that they say here a living truth in their lives. Amen.

———— ℘ ————

Eternal God, creator and preserver of all life,
author of salvation, giver of all grace;
Bless and sanctify with your Holy Spirit
____ and ____, who come now to join in marriage.
Grant that they may give their vows to each other
in the strength of your steadfast love.
Enable them to grow in love and peace
with you and with one another all their days,
that they may reach out
in concern and service to the world
through Jesus Christ our Lord. Amen.

                              —*United Methodist prayer*

———— ℘ ————

(Words in parentheses are optional)

Our God at this sacred moment (in the quiet of your house) we pray for Your blessings upon these Your children. They come into Your presence with precious gifts: (their youth), their love, their hopes and dreams, their faith in each other, and their trust in You. As they consecrate these gifts to Your service, we pray that they may find life's deepest meaning and richest happiness. Bind their lives together, O God, in sanctity and devotion. Teach them to ennoble life as they share their love together. Blessed are you who come here in the name of God. Serve God with gladness; come before God with singing. O God, supremely blessed, supreme in might and glory, guide and bless this bridegroom and this bride.

—*Jewish ceremony*

———— ༀ ————

(This may be spoken or sung by an individual or by the congregation)
     Our Father, who art in heaven, hallowed be thy name. Thy kingdom come. Thy will be done. On earth as it is in heaven. Give us this day our daily bread. And forgive us our trespasses, as we forgive those who trespass against us. Lead us not into temptation, but deliver us from evil. For thine is the kingdom, and the power, and the glory, for ever and ever. Amen.

———— ༀ ————

O eternal God, creator and preserver of all mankind, giver of all spiritual grace, author of everlasting life; send thy blessing upon these thy servants, this man and this woman, whom we bless in thy name, that they, living faithfully together, may surely perform and keep the vow and covenant they have made, and may they ever remain in perfect love and peace together, and live according to thy laws, through Jesus Christ our Lord, Amen.

—*The Book of Common Prayer*

———— ༀ ————

O Lord, open thou our lips, that our mouths may show forth thy praise; open thou our minds, that we may be enlightened by your truth; open thou our hearts, that we may receive the fullness of your grace; open thou the deep river of our spirits, that we may become one with you.

—*Adapted from a Baptist ceremony*

God of all peoples:
You are the true light illuminating everyone.
You show us the way, the truth, and the life.
You show us love even when we are disobedient.
You sustain us with your Spirit.
We rejoice in your life in the midst of our lives.
We praise you for your presence with us,
especially now, and we celebrate and
consecrate this sacred covenant.
—United Methodist prayer

Blessed art Thou, O Lord our God, King of the universe, who hath
created joy and sadness, bridegroom and bride, mirth, exultation,
pleasure and delight, love and brotherhood, and peace and friendship.
O Lord our God, may there soon be heard in the cities of Judah and
in the streets of Jerusalem the voice of joy and the voice of gladness,
the voice of the bridegroom and the voice of the bride, the jubilant
voice of the bridegrooms from their canopies and of youths from
their feasts of song. Blessed are Thou, O Lord, who maketh the bridegroom to rejoice with the bride.
—Jewish prayer

❧ READINGS ❧

The minute I heard my first love story
I started looking for you, not knowing
how blind that was.

Lovers don't finally meet somewhere.
They're in each other all along.
—Rumi

———— ⁓ ————

Sometimes our life reminds me
of a forest in which there is a graceful clearing
and in that opening a house,
an orchard and garden,
comfortable shades, and flowers
red and yellow in the sun, a pattern
made in the light for the light to return to.
The forest is mostly dark, its way
to be made anew day after day, the dark
richer than the light and more blessed
provided we stay brave
enough to keep on going in.
                    —*Wendell Berry, The Country of Marriage*

———— ⁓ ————

Perhaps they were
right putting love
into books
perhaps it could not
live anywhere else.
—*Faulkner*

Love. What a small word we use for an idea so immense and powerful it has altered the flow of history, calmed monsters, kindled
works of art, cheered the forlorn, turned tough guys to mush, consoled the enslaved, driven strong women mad, glorified the humble,
fueled national scandals, bankrupted robber barons, and made mince-
meat of kings. How can love's spaciousness be conveyed in the narrow
confines of one syllable? . . . Love is an ancient delirium, a desire
older than civilization, with taproots stretching deep into dark and
mysterious days. . . .

   The heart is a living museum. In each of its galleries, no matter how
narrow or dimly lit, preserved forever like wondrous diatoms, are
our moments of loving and being loved.
                    —*Diane Ackerman, A History of Love*

———— ⁓ ————

In Chota Nagput and Bengal
the betrothed are tied with threads to
mango trees, they marry the trees

as well as one another, and
the two trees marry each other.
Could we do that sometime with oaks
or beeches? This gossamer we
hold each other with, this web
of love and habit is not enough.
In mistrust of heavier ties,
I would like tree-siblings for us,
standing together somewhere, two
trees married with us, lightly, their
fingers barely touching in sleep,
our threads invisible but holding.

    —*William Meredith, Partial Accounts*

A Marriage

You are holding up a ceiling
with both arms. It is very heavy,
but you must hold it up, or else
it will fall down on you. Your arms
are tired, terribly tired,
and, as the day goes on, it feels
as if either your arms or the ceiling
will soon collapse.

But then,
unexpectedly,
something wonderful happens:
Someone,
a man or a woman,
walks into the room
and holds their arms up
to the ceiling beside you.

So you finally get
to take down your arms.
You feel the relief of respite,
the blood flowing back
to your fingers and arms.
And when you partner's arms tire,
you hold up your own
to relieve him again.

And it can go on like this
for many years
without the house falling.

—*Michael Blumenthal*

⌇

A Prayer for a Wedding
because everyone knows exactly what's good for another
because very few see
because a man and a woman may just possibly look at each other
because in the insanity of human relationships there still
    may come a time we say: yes, yes
because a man or a woman can do anything he or she pleases
because you can reach any point in your life saying: now, I want
    this
because eventually it occurs we want each other, we want
    to know each other, even stupidly, even uglily
because there is at best a simple need in two people to try
    and reach some simple ground
because that simple ground is not so simple
because we are human beings gathered together whether
    we like it or not
because we are human beings reaching out to touch

because sometimes we grow
 we ask a blessing on this marriage
 we ask that some simplicity be allowed
 we ask their happiness
 we ask that this couple be known for what it is,
 and that the light shine upon it
 we ask a blessing for their marriage
    —Joel Oppenheimer

The Blind Leading the Blind

Take my hand. There are two of us in this cave.
The sound you hear is water; you will hear it forever.
The ground you walk on is rock. I have been here before.
People come here to be born, to discover, to kiss,
to dream and to dig and to kill. Watch for the mud.
Summer blows in with scent of horses and roses;
fall with the sound of sound breaking; winter shoves
its empty sleeve down the dark of your throat.
You will learn toads from diamonds, the fist from the palm,
love from the sweat of love, falling from flying.
There are a thousand turnoffs. I have been here before.
Once I fell off a precipice. Once I found gold.
Once I stumbled on murder, the thin parts of a girl.
Walk on, keep walking, there are axes above us.
Watch for occasional bits and bubbles of light—
birthdays for you, recognitions: yourself, another.
Watch for the mud. Listen for bells, for beggars.
Something with wings went crazy against my chest once.
There are two of us here. Touch me.
    —Lisel Mueller

———— ৯ ————

Then Almitra spoke again and said, And what of Marriage,
    master?
And he answered saying:
You were born together, and together you shall be for ever more.
You shall be together when the white wings of death scatter your
    days.
Aye, you shall be together even in the silent memory of God.
But let there be spaces in your togetherness.
And let the winds of heavens dance between you.

Love one another, but make not a bond of love:
Let it rather be a moving sea between the shores of your souls.
Fill each other's cup but drink not from one cup.
Give one another of your bread but eat not from the same loaf.
Sing and dance together and be joyous, but let each one of you
    be alone,
Even as the strings of a lute are alone though they quiver with the
    same music.
Give your hearts, but not into each other's keeping.
For only the hand of Life can contain your hearts.
And stand together yet not too near together:
For the pillars of the temple stand apart,
And the oak tree and the cypress grow not in each other's shadow.
                    —*Kahlil Gibran, The Prophet*

———— ৯ ————

Love's Philosophy
The Fountains mingle with the River
    And the Rivers with the Oceans,
The winds of Heaven mix forever
    With a sweet emotion;
Nothing in the world is single;
    All things by a law divine
In one spirit meet and mingle.
    Why not I with thine?—

See the mountains kiss high Heaven
    And the waves clasp one another;
No sister-flower would be forgiven
    If it disdained its brother,
And the sunlight clasps the earth
    And the moonbeams kiss the sea:
What is all this sweet work worth
    If thou kiss not me?
                —*Percy Bysshe Shelley*

The Place Poem—3

I could open the doors
    and the windows
to great winds.
   let everything be scattered
like
   loose
     sheets of paper.
let tumbling take sense and
proportion from what we have
put in order
    that suits us.
but it would not change
      anything.
You have come in,
    and your entrance
has been final.
    You do not leave me,
nor do I leave you, beloved.
We have made of this house
our place
   and our shelter.
When we go out, we will go out
   together.
                —*Ted Enslin*

Love Comes Quietly

Love comes quietly,
finally, drops
about me, on me,
in the old ways.

What did I know
thinking myself
able to go
alone all the way
                    —*Robert Creeley*

Taking the Hands

Taking the hands of someone you love,
You see they are delicate cages . . .
Tiny birds are singing
In the secluded prairies
And in the deep valleys of the hand.
                    —*Robert Bly*

Hymn to the Sun

O Morning Star! When you look down
upon us, give us peace and refreshing sleep.

Great Spirit! Bless our children, friends, and
visitors through a happy life.

May our trails lie straight and level before
us. Let us live to behold. We are all your
children and ask these things with good hearts.
                    —*Great Plains Indians*

⁓

Hindu Marriage Poem
You have become mine forever.
Yes, we have become partners.
I have become yours.
Hereafter, I cannot live without you.
Do not live without me.
Let us share the joys.
We are word and meaning, united.
You are thought and I am sound.

May the nights be honey-sweet for us.
May the mornings be honey-sweet for us.
May the plants be honey-sweet for us.
May the earth be honey-sweet for us.

⁓

For love is as strong as death.

I hear my Beloved. See how he comes
leaping on the mountains,
bounding over the hills.
My Beloved is like a gazelle,
like a young stag.

See where he stands behind our wall.
He looks in at the window,
he peers through the lattice.

My Beloved lifts up his voice, he says to me,
"Come then, my love,
my lovely, come.

"My dove, hiding in the clefts of the rock,
in the coverts of the cliff,
show me your face,
let me hear your voice;
for your voice is sweet
and your face is beautiful."

My Beloved is mine and I am his.
He said to me:
'Set me like a seal on your heart,
like a seal on your arm.
For love is strong as Death,
jealousy relentless as Sheol.
The flash of it is a flash of fir,
a flame of the Lord himself.'

Love no flood can quench,
no torrents drown.

> —*The Jerusalem Bible, Song of Songs 2:8–10,*
> *14, 16a; 8:6–7a*

I do not offer the old smooth prizes,
But offer rough new prizes,
These are the days that must happen to you:
You shall not heap up what is called riches,
You shall scatter with lavish hand all that you earn or achieve.
However sweet the laid-up stores,
However convenient the dwellings,
You shall not remain there.
However sheltered the port,
And however calm the waters,
You shall not anchor there.

However welcome the hospitality that welcomes you
You are permitted to receive it but a little while
Afoot and lighthearted, take to the open road,
Healthy, free, the world before you,
The long brown path before you, leading wherever
you choose.
Say only to one another:
Camerado, I give you my hand!
I give you my love, more precious than money,
I give you myself before preaching or law:
Will you give me yourself?
Will you come travel with me?
Shall we stick by each other as long as we live?
> —*Walt Whitman*

What is the beginning? Love.
What the course. Love still.
What the goal. The goal is Love.

On a happy hill
Is there nothing then but Love?
Search we sky or earth
There is nothing out of Love
Hath perpetual worth:
All things flag but only Love,
All things fail and flee;
There is nothing left but Love
Worthy you and me.
> —*Christina Rossetti*

So Much Happiness

It is difficult to know what to do with so much happiness.
With sadness there is something to rub against,
a wound to tend with lotion and cloth.
When the world falls in around you, you have pieces to pick up,
something to hold in your hands, like ticket stubs or change.

But happiness floats.
It doesn't need you to hold it down.
It doesn't need anything.
Happiness lands on the roof of the next house, singing,
and disappears when it wants to.
You are happy either way.
Even the fact that you once lived in a peaceful tree house
and now live over a quarry of noise and dust
cannot make you unhappy.
Everything has a life of its own,
it too could wake up filled with possibilities
of coffee cake and ripe peaches,
and love even the floor which needs to be swept,
the soiled linens and scratched records . . .

Since there is no place large enough
to contain so much happiness,
you shrug, you raise your hands, and it flows out of you
into everything you touch. You are not responsible.
You take no credit, as the night sky takes no credit
for the moon, but continues to hold it, and share it,
and in that way, be known.

      —Naomi Shihab Nye

I love you,
Not only for what you are
But for what I am
When I am with you.

I love you,
Not only for what
You have made of yourself
But for what
You are making of me.

I love you,
For the part of me
That you bring out;
I love you,
For putting your hand
Into my heaped-up heart
And passing over
All the foolish, weak things
That you can't help
Dimly seeing there,
And for drawing out
Into the light
All the beautiful belongings
That no one else had looked
Quite far enough to find.

I love you because you
Are helping me to make
Of the lumber of my life
Not a tavern

But a temple;
Out of works
Of my every day
Not a reproach
But a song.

—*Roy Croft*

—————— ✧ ——————

Epithalamion
If you, X, take this woman, Y,
and if you, Y, take this man, X,
you two who have taken each other
many times before, then this
is something to be trusted,

two separate folks not becoming halves,
as younger people do, but becoming neither more nor less
    than yourselves,
separate and together, and if
this means a different kind of love,

as it must, if it means different
conveniences and inconveniences, as it must,
then let this good luck
from a friend act like grease
for what may yet be difficult, undefined,

and when the ordinary days of marriage
stretch out like prairie,
here's to the wisdom which understands
that if the heart's right
and the mind at ease with it
the prairie is a livable place, a place
for withstanding all kinds of weather,

and here's to the little hills,
the ones that take you by surprise,
and the ones you'll need to invent.
                    —*Stephen Dunn*

———— ꙮ ————

Psalm I
Blessed are the man and the woman
    who have grown beyond themselves
    and have seen through their separations.
They delight in the way things are
    and keep their hearts open, day and night.
They are like trees planted near flowing rivers,
    which bear fruit when they are ready.
Their leaves will not fall or wither.
        Everything they do will succeed.
                    —*The book of Psalms,*
                    adapted by Stephen Mitchell

———— ꙮ ————

Sonnet XVII
I don't love you as if you were the salt-rose, topaz
or arrow of carnations that propagate fire:
I love you as certain dark things are loved,
secretly, between the shadow and the soul.

I love you as the plant that doesn't bloom and carries
hidden within itself the light of those flowers,
and thanks to your love, darkly in my body
lives dense fragrance that rises from the earth.

I love you without knowing how, or when, or from where,
I love you simply, without problems or pride:
I love you in this way because I don't know any other way
    of loving

but this, in which there is no I or you,
so intimate that your hand upon my chest is my hand,
so intimate that when I fall asleep it is your eyes that close.
                    —*Pablo Neruda, translated by Stephen Mitchell*

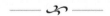

Sonnet XLVIII
Two happy lovers make one single bread,
one single drop of moonlight in the grass.
When they walk, they leave two shadows that merge,
and they leave one single sun blazing in their bed.
                    —*Pablo Neruda, translated by Stephen Mitchell*

Go deeper than love, for the soul has greater depths,
love is like the grass, but the heart is deep wild rock
molten, yet dense and permanent.

Go down to your deep old heart, and lose sight of yourself.
And lose sight of me, the me whom you turbulently loved.

Let us lose sight of ourselves, and break the mirrors.
For the fierce curve of our lives is moving again to the depths
out of sight, in the deep living heart.
                    —*D. H. Lawrence, from "Know Deeply, Know
                    Thyself More Deeply"*

For one human being to love another human being: that is perhaps
the most difficult task that has been entrusted to us, the ultimate
task, the final test and proof, the work for which all other work is
merely preparation. Loving does not at first mean merging, surren-
dering, and uniting with another person—it is a high inducement for
the individual to ripen, to become something in himself, to become
world, to become world in himself for the sake of another person; it

is a great, demanding claim on him, something that chooses him and calls him to vast distance. . . .

Once the realization is accepted that even between the closest people infinite distances exist, a marvelous living side-by-side can grow up for them, if they succeed in loving the expanse between them, which gives them the possibility of seeing each other as a whole and before an immense sky.

—*Rainer Maria Rilke*

———— ✲ ————

Now you will feel no rain,
for each of you will be a shelter to the other.

Now you will feel no cold,
for each of you will be warmth to the other.

Now there is no loneliness for you;
now there is no more loneliness.

Now you are two bodies,
but there is only one life before you.

Go now to your dwelling place
to enter into your days together.

And may your days be good
and long on the earth.

—*Apache song*

———— ✲ ————

Love is a great thing, a great good in every way; it alone lightens what is heavy, and leads smoothly over all roughness. For it carries a burden without being burdened, and makes every bitter thing sweet and tasty. Love wants to be lifted up, not held back by anything low. Love wants to be free, and far from all worldly desires, so that its inner vision may not be dimmed and good fortune bind it or misfortune cast it down. Nothing is sweeter than love; nothing stronger, nothing higher, nothing wider; nothing happier, nothing fuller, nothing better in heaven and earth; for love is born of God . . .

Love keeps watch and is never unaware, even when it sleeps; tired, it is never exhausted; hindered, it is never defeated; alarmed, it is never afraid; but like a living flame and a burning torch it bursts upward and blazes forth . . .

Love is quick, sincere, dutiful, joyous, and pleasant; brave, patient, faithful, prudent, serene, and vigorous; and it never seeks itself. For whenever we seek ourselves, we fall away from love. Love is watchful, humble, and upright; not weak, or frivolous, or directed toward vain things; temperate, pure, steady, calm, and alert in all the senses. Love is devoted and thankful to God, always trusting and hoping in him, even when it doesn't taste his sweetness, for without pain no one can live in love.

—Thomas à Kempis, translated by Stephen Mitchell

Here all seeking is over,
the lost has been found,
a mate has been found
to share the chills of winter—
now Love asks
that you be united.
Here is a place to rest,
a place to sleep,
a place in heaven.
Now two are becoming one,
the black night is scattered,
the eastern sky grows bright.
At last the great day has come!

—Hawaiian song

You and I
Have so much love
That it
Burns like a fire,
In which we bake a lump of clay
Molded into a figure of you
And a figure of me.
Then we take both of them,
and break them into pieces,
And mix the pieces with water,
And mold again a figure of you,
And a figure of me.
I am in your clay.
You are in my clay.
In life we share a single quilt.
In death we will share one bed.
                    —*Kuan Tao-Sheng, translated by Kenneth*
                    Rexroth and Ling Chung

❧ VOWS ❧

All that I am and all that I have
I offer to you, my beloved,
     in joy
     in service
     in sacred union.

All that I dream and all I desire
I ask from you, my beloved,
     in thanksgiving
     in anticipation
     in celebration.

All that I need and all that is broken
in me I present to you, my beloved,
>   for your healing
>   for your nurturing and mending
>   for your soothing love.

All that I have been and all that I shall be
I bring into your midst, my beloved,
>   for your blessing
>   for your clear reflection
>   for your sacred witness.

All that I am and all that I have
I entrust to your heart, my beloved,
>   on this sacred day
>   and tomorrow
>   and always.

———— ৵ ————

I, ___,
choose you, ___,
in the presence of this community,
to be my wife/husband/spouse/partner,
from this time forward.
To love you,
To be a comfort and safe haven in your life,
To hold you close,
To listen deeply when you are sad or angry,
To learn compassion with you,
To nourish you with my gentleness, to uphold you with my strength,
To love your body as it ages,
To weigh the effects of the words I speak and of the things I do,
To never take you for granted, but always give thanks for your
>   presence.

As our lives unfold together,
I promise to be faithful,
To always express my emotional truth and
embrace you as both teacher and student as we do what
    life calls us to,
individually and in relationship.

———— ✍ ————

These, my love, are my promises to you:
that I will love you freely,
    as the sky loves the bird,
    as the sunset loves the early evening.
That I will love you grandly,
    with my tender fine emotions,
    with my loving words and all my actions.
That I will love you purely,
    with my honor, with my knowing,
    with all the best intentions of my being.
That I will love you joyfully,
    with my body, with my laughter,
    with my foolishness and playing.
That I will love you truly,
    with my finest kindness and my deepest care.
That I will love you always,
    now, from this day forward,
    seamless, endless, and forever.

———— ✍ ————

I give you my love
I give you my heart
I give you my hope
I give you with joy
    from the coffers of my precious time
    the rest of the days of my life;

To delight in your body
To nourish your mind
To be at home with your spirit
    the way a star is at home in the sky;
To celebrate your whole being with joy
    as the sun emblazons the sea
    with its light;
To know you, love you, hold you, warm you
Through all the long days of our lives.

—— ๖ ——

Until we both shall grow old
    and the sight fall
    from our eyes and our being
    fall from life to light;
I choose to go with you always
from this day until the end of our days
as your adoring husband (wife/mate).

—— ๖ ——

In the name of God,
I ____ take you ____
to be my beloved wife (husband/mate).

To stand with you in the grand love that binds us,
to honor you, to change with you,
to behold the highest meanings of our being,
to learn compassion with you,
to suffer with you,
to rejoice, to be kind.

I promise you this
from my heart
with my soul
till death do us part.

—— ✺ ——

Because I have never known such a love
I take you now, for forever
to be my dear husband (wife).

I long to know you,
I desire to discover you.
I promise always to honor you, to mirror
you in the beautiful uniqueness of your spirit,
to thank you when you delight me,
to forgive you when you offend me,
to receive you as the fulfillment
of all my lessons
the chalice of all my joy.

Therefore, do I give myself to you now
in this consecrated state of being married,
to hold you in my heart, to protect you
with the wings of my soul, to be blessed
by the gift of your love
for all the days of my life.

—— ✺ ——

Before God and these our witnesses,
this is my solemn promise:
to love you and hold you always
    as my wife (husband);
to stand beside you in good times
and bad
because my love is so great, and
your presence such a miracle;
to be sweet with you and fierce
    with you,

to nourish you with my gentleness,
to uphold you with my strength,
to go with you through the
    changes of age and infirmity,
whatever the sorrows or losses,
until we become pure spirits
in the end.

———— ℘ ————

My love
I waited so long for you
that I had begun to believe
there was no such thing as true love,
that my life would be lived out
alone, that nothing precious
would come in the form
of someone to love.

Finally, after so many sorrows
    and missteps and losses,
after I had given up all hope,
you were given to me like
a miracle, like a single
elegant star in the darkest
of nights.

Now I feel joy
Now I feel whole
Now I feel that anything
is possible.

Thank you for coming
into my life; thank you
for loving me well.
I have waited so long for my heart

to be glad, for my soul
to be full.

Thank you for coming
into my life. Thank you
for coming into
my love.

———— ✤ ————

I, ____, take you, ____,
from this day forward and into
the long forever to be my beloved,
my sweetheart, my darling, my wife (husband/mate).

I promise always to love you,
to honor you, to adore you,
to give thanks for the gift
of your presence.
You are the one I admire;
You are the one I adore.
You are the one I choose
to go on with forever,
from now until the end
of my life.

———— ✤ ————

Startled awake
at this late and unexpectedly beautiful
hour, long after sorrow, long after
love, long after hope,
I receive you into the breath
of my soul
to make my light with you,
to fill with joy my glad heart,
and to love you far more and dearly

than ever before in all your
imaginings you could have imagined;

with the sight of my eyes, with
the wings of my heart, with
the milk of my soul.

I have come to you
with the plain grace
of a small bird
to love you
and I will
love you:

honor you and adore you,
and with my body console
you, and with my mind embrace
the unrepeatable refinements
of your being.
So will I love you,
so will I your father mother sister brother
   lover son and daughter be,
soul of your soul will I, kin of your kin be
in sleeksilver weather and greybleeding times.
I will keepsake your heart in my soul, in
the palms of my eyes in the small
of my hand;

I will love you
as the hawk flies high and floating circle
in the blue sky bowled intelligent
and endlessly alive above us,
till the wingspan stilled falls
and the new night starry bright
incomprehensible and distant

beautifully bows down
and frees us from the earth
sun moon sky
and takes us wakes us
and as stars we are reborn.

———— ✌ ————

I, ___, take you, ___,
To be my beloved wife (husband/mate)
To give you, from this day forward, the gift of my tender love
To honor you with my body
To fill up the wounds in your heart;
To sleep in your bed and stand at your side
In good times and bad
When things go easy with us
and also when they are difficult;

When love is a gift
and when it is an effort;
When we are successful and prosperous
and when the wolf of uncertainty lurks at the door.

I promise always
    to love you
    to cherish you
    to hold you always in highest regard, and
    to die with this love that I have for you
    untarnished in my heart.

———— ✌ ————

Now do I marry you,
now do I take you forever
into my heart, and loving you now
I promise that I shall be steadfast
always in my love.

You are my princess, my darling, my queen
   (my prince, my knight, my king)

my companion, my consort, my jester,
   my most highly honored person,
So do I choose you, so do I love you,
so do I promise, from this day forward
to be your most cherishing husband (wife/mate).

———— ॐ ————

____, my beloved,
I choose now to take this journey
   with you
wherever it leads
whatever the outcome
no matter what may befall us
as God is my witness
through all the days
of our lives.

———— ॐ ————

I, ____, take you, ____,
to be my partner in marriage
and in life

To love you and honor you
To give thanks for you and
To serve you
   with my wit
   my strength
   my heart
To stand by you always
   even if sickness should threaten
   and despite the turmoil around us

To create with you a living example
of the beauty of a relationship
between a man and a woman.

I promise always to listen to you
To labor with you
To encourage you

To believe in you even
    when you doubt yourself
To be the mirror
    of your highest value
And to hold myself beside you
until the gates of death.

In the past, in a world defined primarily by masculine consciousness, by the values of aggression, formality, and contracts, even in marriage we tended to make straightforward, contractual promises. A woman offered her dowry; a man his support. A woman promised to love and obey; a man promised to love and provide. Here is a vow that, instead of promising to fulfill an obligation, comes forward in vulnerability to ask your beloved to give you what you need.

You may want to use it as presented here, or as a blueprint to *fashion some heartfelt requests of your own.*

My Beloved,
In this world where everything is changing, where everything old is falling away, and everything new is coming swiftly into being, I, ____, choose you, ____, to be my companion, my lover, my wife (husband).

I pledge my heart and the unfolding of my life to you, and I ask you to stand at my side at the turn of every corner, in the midst of each unveiling.

It is you to whom I have come for comfort in the past, you from whom I shall ask for solace in the future. It is you who have held me up, you whom I now ask to hold me and enfold me in the long tomorrow.

I ask for your care and comfort and love.
I ask for your wisdom and truth.
I ask for your patience and kindness.
I ask you to listen to me; to allow me to bring all my sorrows to
     you, my confusion, my tribulations; to honor me in the tender
     place of my fragile emotions.

I ask you to share in my joys, to celebrate my victories, to rejoice in all my achievements, and never to rain on my parade.

I ask you to measure your words, to speak to me thoughtfully, with care, in consciousness, knowing the power of words to wound.

I bring you my body as a fine gift; I ask you to honor it, to nurture it with your love, to enjoy my essence, my spirit, which deeply resides within it, to love me still as it ages, to allow me to honor you, also, in every gracious way with it.

I ask you to bring your deep spirit to this marriage, your willingness to walk the path of surrender, of spiritual seeking and finding.

I choose to make my whole life with you, ____, because you are the man (woman) I adore; the being above all others who has been sent here to be a gift to me, to be now and always my love.

Officiant: ____, will you have this woman (man) to be thy lawful wedded wife (husband/partner/spouse), to live together after God's ordinance in the holy estate of matrimony? Will you love her (him), comfort her (him), honor and keep her (him) in sickness and in health; and, forsaking all others, keep thee only unto her (him), so long as ye both shall live?

Response: I, ____, take thee/you, ____, to be my wedded wife (husband), to have and to hold from this day forward, for better for worse, for richer for poorer, in sickness and in health, to love and to cherish, till death do us part, according to God's holy ordinance; and thereto I plight thee/you my troth.

—The Book of Common Prayer

———— ♾ ————

Officiant: Do you, ____, take this woman (man), ____, to be your wedded wife (husband); and do you, in the presence of God and before these witnesses, promise and covenant to be to her (him) a loving, faithful, and dutiful husband (wife) unto thee, until God shall separate you by death?"

Response: I do.

—Church of Scotland

———— ♾ ————

Officiant: ____, will you have ____ to be your wedded wife (husband/spouse/partner), to live together in the covenant of faith, hope, and love according to the intention of God for your lives? Will you listen to her (his) deepest thoughts, be tender-hearted and kind/wise in your daily care of her (him), and stand faithfully at her (his) side in sickness and in health? Choosing her (him) above all others, will you undertake to care for her (his) well-being of mind and body and spirit, as long as you both shall live?

Response: I will.

—Adapted from a Baptist ceremony

———— ♾ ————

I betroth you to me forever;
I betroth you to me with steadfast love and compassion,
I betroth you to me in faithfulness.

—Hosea 2:21–22, sometimes said in
Jewish ceremonies

If love is the answer,
could you please
rephrase the question?
—Lily Tomlin

———— ⁂ ————

In the name of God,
I, ____, take you, ____,
to be my wife (husband),
to have and to hold
from this day onward,
for better for worse,
for richer for poorer,
in sickness and in health,
to love and to cherish,
until we are parted by death.
This is my solemn vow.
                    —*Methodist ceremony*

❧ BLESSING OF THE RINGS ❧

For the man:
This wedding band, a perfect circle of precious metal, symbolizes a man's kingdom and all his worldly possessions. As you join together in marriage, you, ____ entrust the riches of your life to ____'s care, that she may be the queen at your side, the honored guest to partake with you of all your worldly blessings, and may she, in return, offer to you the wisdom of her heart, the secrets of her soul, for your spiritual safekeeping, knowing always that she is encircled by your love.

For the woman:
This wedding band, a perfect circle of precious metal, symbolizes a woman's riches, the knowing of her heart, her beauty, her intuition, her deep emotional wisdom. ____, as you join ____ in marriage, you are offering your spiritual wisdom, that he may be the king at your side, the man protected by your love, and may he, in perfect safety, offer to you all the sorrows of his heart, the secrets of his soul, for your spiritual safekeeping, knowing always that he is encircled by your love.

In the past, rings were a symbol of bondage, of who was enslaved to whom. These rings are a redemption of that symbol, a sign of bonding in freedom, of your having chosen to cast your lot with one another in this life, and of the seamless circle of joy that surrounds you both.

As a token of the covenant into which you have entered, this ring is given and received.

—*Church of Scotland*

Bless, O Lord, this ring to be a sign of the vows by which this man and this woman have bound themselves to one other.

—*Roman Catholic ceremony*

Lord, bless and consecrate ____ and ____ in their love for each other. May these rings be a symbol of true faith in each other and always remind them of their love. Through Christ our Lord. Amen.

—*Roman Catholic ceremony*

Lord,
bless these rings which we bless in your name.
Grant that those who wear them
may always have a deep faith in each other.
May they do your will
and always live together
in peace, good will, and love.
We ask this through Christ our Lord.

—*Roman Catholic ceremony*

———— ✤ ————

Bless, O Lord, this ring, that he who gives and she who wears it may abide in thy peace and continue in thy favor, unto their life's end through Jesus Christ our Lord. Amen.
—*The Book of Common Prayer*

———— ✤ ————

These rings
are the outward and visible sign
of an inward and spiritual grace,
signifying to us the union
between Jesus Christ and his Church.
—*United Methodist ceremony*

✤ EXCHANGING OF THE RINGS ✤

As the sign from my heart
that I desire to live with you
from this day forward as my wife (husband/mate),
and that you may remember forever
that I have chosen you above all others,
I give you this ring as a sign of my love.

———— ✤ ————

This ring is my precious gift to you,
as a measure of my love and as a sign
that from this day forward your every breath
shall be surrounded by my love.

———— ✤ ————

I give you this ring as a sign
that I choose you to be my beloved,
and that I offer myself as your husband (wife)
today, tomorrow, and always.

—— ꙅ ——

I marry you with this ring,
with my heart,
with my body,
and with all the syllables
of my soul.

—— ꙅ ——

As a symbol
of how endlessly happy you make me
and of how crazy I am about you,
I give you this ring, my dear sweetheart,
so you and the whole world will know
how much and how always I love you.

—— ꙅ ——

I give you this ring
as the symbol that
I have cast my lot with
yours, that I am bound
to you always, through my love,
with my soul, and all my heart.

—— ꙅ ——

This ring is a token of my endless and abiding love, because it is you,
____, whom I love, and it is you whom I am choosing always to
encircle with my love.
Wear it in health,
Wear it in joy
Wear it in peace
Wear it in bliss.
Wear this ring in health
    because you have healed me

Wear it in joy
  because you have made my heart glad
Wear it in peace
  because you have brought me serenity
Wear it in bliss
  because you have brought me true grace.

———— ℘ ————

I hope you will wear this ring as a reminder
that *I love you*
every single day of your life.

———— ℘ ————

I love you, ____. Here, this is my ring. Can we go steady for life?

———— ℘ ————

Darling, I ask you to receive this ring as a symbol of my love and as a constant reminder that I have chosen you above all others to be the one to share my life.

———— ℘ ————

May this ring be the sign, always, that we love one another.

  May it be the symbol, always, that we have chosen to serve one another in perfect freedom.

  May it be the public demonstration that our love is complete and never ending.

  May it be the object that tells, when we as ourselves are no more and our bones have crumbled to dust, that our love in this life was real and eternal and deep.

———— ℘ ————

____, I give you this ring as a symbol of my vow, and with all that I am, and I that I have, I honor you.

—Adapted from a Protestant ceremony

———— ✌ ————

Receive this ring as a token of wedding love and troth.
—*Lutheran ceremony*

———— ✌ ————

With this ring I thee wed, in the name of the Father, and of the Son, and of the Holy Ghost. Amen.
—*The Book of Common Prayer*

———— ✌ ————

Behold thou art consecrated to me with this ring, according to the Law of Moses and of Israel.
—*Act of espousal recited by Jewish bridegroom while placing ring on bride's right forefinger*

———— ✌ ————

In the Church of Scotland ceremony, the couple do not speak at the exchanging of rings. Rather, as the couple places the rings on their fingers and then hold hands, the officiant says:

By this sign you take each other, to have and to hold, from this day forward, for better, for worse, for richer, for poorer; in sickness and in health; to love and to cherish, till death do you part.

❧ PRONOUNCEMENT OF MARRIAGE ☙

Because, ____ and ____, you have showered our hearts with expressions of your love, and promised each other the joy of all your days, it gives me great honor and pleasure to now pronounce you husband and wife.

———— ✌ ————

Because you, ____ and ____, have come together with your hearts and minds and souls, and pledged one another the future in holy matrimony, I now pronounce you husband and wife.

—— ✲ ——

Because ____ and ____ have pledged their love and commitment to each other before these witnesses, I declare that they are husband and wife. May the Spirit that lives in and around all of us fill your hearts and bless your lives.

—— ✲ ——

For as much as ____ and ____ have consented together in holy wedlock, and have witnessed the same before God and in this company, and have committed themselves wholeheartedly to one another, and have expressed this through the symbol of their rings, I now pronounce them husband and wife.

—Adapted from a Baptist ceremony

—— ✲ ——

For as much as ____ and ____ have consented together in holy wedlock, and have witnessed the same before God and this company, and thereto have given and pledged their troth, each to the other, and have declared the same by giving and receiving a ring and by joining hands; I pronounce that they are man and wife, in the name of the Father, and of the Son, and of the Holy Ghost. Amen.

—The Book of Common Prayer

✤ BENEDICTION ✤

May you be blessed, every step of your path by the great god of light. May the sun shine upon you; may the moon move the tide of your emotions with every grace and magic; may your hearts sing; may your hearth be warm; and may your every blessed day be filled with joy.

—— ✲ ——

Go in peace, dear ones, for God has given you the greatest of all gifts, true love, love embodied, love promised and sworn, love twined to itself till death do you part.

May every word you speak and every breath you take in each other's presence, be twice blessed, truth and joy, and may you walk together in strength each holy day of your lives.

Go in peace, for you, together, have done the beautiful thing.

———— ⟡ ————

He who is mighty above all beings
He who is blessed above all beings,
He who is great above all beings,
May he bless the bridegroom and the bride.

—Medieval hymn, often used in Jewish weddings

———— ⟡ ————

May God be gracious unto you and bless you and make his face to shine upon you always.

—Baptist ceremony

———— ⟡ ————

The Lord bless thee and keep thee. The Lord make his face shine upon thee, and be gracious unto thee. The Lord lift up his countenance upon thee, and give thee peace.

—Lutheran ceremony

———— ⟡ ————

God the father, God the Son, God the Holy Ghost, bless, preserve, and keep you; the Lord mercifully with his favor look upon you, and fill you will all spiritual benediction and grace; that you may so live together in this life, that in the world to come you may have life everlasting. Amen.

—The Book of Common Prayer

———— ⟡ ————

God Almighty send you his light and truth to keep you all the days of your life. The hand of God protect you; his holy Angels accompany you. God the Father, God the Son, and God the Holy Ghost cause his grace to be mighty upon you.

—Lutheran ceremony

———— ✌ ————

And now I ask you and all your dear ones to bow your heads in reverence. Silently let us pray that God will bless your home and help you achieve your highest hopes.

—Jewish benediction

———— ✌ ————

God the Eternal, keep you in love with each other
so that the peace of Christ may abide in your home
Go to serve God and your neighbor in all that you do.

Bear witness to the love of God in this world
so that those to whom love is a stranger
will find in you generous friends.
The grace of the Lord Jesus Christ,
and the love of God,
and the communion of the Holy Spirit
be with you, now and always.

—United Methodist ceremony

———— ✌ ————

The peace of God, which passes all understanding, keep your hearts and minds in the knowledge and love of God, and of His Son, Jesus Christ our Lord; and the blessings of God Almighty, the Father, the Son, and the Holy Spirit, be upon you, and remain with you always.

—Church of Scotland

———— ✌ ————

God the eternal Father keep you in love with each other,
so that the peace of Christ may stay with you
and be always in your home.

Response: Amen.

May (your children bless you,)
your friends console you,
and all humans live in peace with you.
Response: Amen.

May you always bear witness to the love of God in this world
so that the afflicted and the needy
will find in you generous friends,
and welcome you into the joys of heaven.
Response: Amen.

And may Almighty God bless you all,
the Father, and the Son, and the Holy Spirit.
Response: Amen.
—Roman Catholic blessing

———— ɔ̃ ————

After the exchanging of the rings and the pronouncement of marriage, you may want the officiant to invite the blessing of the guests on your behalf. You could have him or her say something like:
We celebrate your union and pray God's blessing upon you.

then turn to the congregation and say:
Will all of you—parents, friends, and witnesses—do everything you can to honor, uphold and care for ____ and ____ as they walk the sacred path of marriage?"
Response: We will.
—Adapted from a Baptist ceremony

———— ɔ̃ ————

Or, the congregation may say:
May the god of light bless your union;
May you find peace in your place in the universe
and in our midst.
May you feel the love of each other always.
Go in peace.

TRADITIONAL
CUSTOMS
from AROUND
the WORLD

E{VERY CULTURE, COUNTRY, AND RELIGIOUS FAITH} has its own unique wedding traditions. These not only reflect a particular cultural or religious outlook, but also embody a symbolic representation of the meaning of love and marriage. You may want to include one of these customs or an adaptation of it in your wedding because it represents an homage to your own roots or simply because it touches your heart. There are, of course, a great many customs that I have not included here, but the ones I've selected seem to speak most directly to the condition of our times, the contemporary longings of our hearts. They are also most adaptable to the wedding ceremonies in this book.

❧ THE WEDDING TREE ❧

Before, during, or after your wedding ceremony, plant a tree, either at your home or in some public place. The planting of a tree represents not only new life, but life continuing. As the tree grows in height, strength, and visibility, it symbolizes the maturing of your love. The custom of planting a wedding tree comes to us from Bermuda, where newlyweds traditionally plant a small tree in their garden.

❧ BREAKING A GLASS ❧

The traditional Jewish wedding ceremony includes a "breaking of the glass." Here the groom, having been offered a glass on a wooden pallet or wrapped in a cloth napkin, smashes it with his foot. The breaking of the glass symbolizes the fragility of life, the fact that whatever we see before us as whole can be rendered broken at any moment. It calls our attention to the need for care toward one another; for just as a glass can be shattered with a single blow, so the grace of the marriage bond can be destroyed with a single infidelity or repeated large or small acts of emotional irresponsibility.

❧ THE CHINESE WEDDING GOBLET ❧

In the traditional Chinese ceremony, the bride and groom are presented with two goblets of honey and wine that are tied together with a red ribbon. At some point in the ceremony, they drink together from the goblets. In the Chinese symbology of color, red is the color of courage and of joy. Thus, the sharing of the wedding cup means that in marriage the bride and groom are coming together not only in the joy of love, but also in the courage it will inevitably require.

❧ THE FLOWER-STREWN PATH ❧

In the past in England, a bride and her bridesmaids would walk to the church on a path strewn with flowers. This is a lovely, colorful (and fragrant) tradition that can be carried out in the aisle of your church, on the outside steps, or in any meadow or mountaintop on which you may choose to get married.

What is symbolized here is the wish that the bride's path through life be like "a bed of roses"—a life of ease and grace. Also, the extravagance of "wasting" the flowers by walking on them symbolizes the wish that life may be so full and easy that the bride and groom may pass through it as if tiptoeing on flowers.

❧ BOTH IN WHITE ❧

You may have already decided to wear white. If you have, it may further your appreciation of your choice to know what this can symbolize. In the Jewish tradition it is believed that when a man marries, his sins are forgiven. Like the holiday of Yom Kippur, marriage is thought to bring atonement for all past wrongdoing. Thus the wedding day is supremely sacred, for the bride and groom who are seen to embark upon married life in a state of utter purity embody in ritual the words of the ancient prophet Isaiah: "Though your sins be as scarlet, they shall be whiter than snow." In reflection of this, both the bride and groom may choose to wear white.

❧ A WEDDING CUP ❧

In an old French custom, the bride and groom drink a toast from a two-handled cup. This, of course, stands for the coming together of their two lives, as a cup is often the symbol of the cup of life. In the French tradition this special cup is called the coupe de mariage; it is often handed down as a heirloom to the next generation of brides and grooms.

❧ WEDDING CANDLES ❧

In both Greece and Germany, the bride and groom traditionally greet one another with candles festooned with ribbons and flowers. These symbolize not only the love and delight with which the man and woman are coming together in marriage, but also the illumination they will bring to one another.

The only thing you have to offer another human being, ever, is your own state of being.

—*Ram Dass*

❧ THE THRONES OF BLESSING ❧

In the Netherlands both bride and groom sit on grand chairs, or thrones, under a canopy of green boughs. There, together, they receive the well-wishes of family and friends. This custom, symbolizing the evergreen freshness and vitality of love, is usually the high point of a pre-wedding gathering. It sends the bride and groom off to their wedding awash in good wishes, blessed and encouraged in their undertaking. Although this is traditionally a pre-wedding tradition, some form of it could be included at the rehearsal dinner or as a part of the reception festivities.

❧ THE TWO-BOUQUET CEREMONY ❧

In Burma both the bride and the groom hold flower bouquets during the recitation of their vows. The symbolism here is that the blessings and obligations of marriage apply to both bride and groom; the promises they make to each other are as precious to the man as they are to the woman. When they have finished their vows, the bride and groom dip their hands in a shared bowl of water, to symbolize the water of life.

❧ A CANOPY OF LOVE ❧

In the Jewish wedding, the ceremony takes place under a beautiful silk or velvet canopy, or huppah. This represents the home that the bride and groom are creating, and, during the ceremony itself, provides the sacred environment in which the bride and groom exchange their rings and take their vows.

Although you may not want an actual huppah, per se, you may want to build on this lovely tradition by featuring a beautiful arch or gazebo decorated with flowers, or a colorful tent in which to conduct your ceremony.

❧ CONFETTI OF FLOWERS ❧

In India, where the fragrance of flowers in the form of incense is deeply a part of spiritual life, the groom's brother traditionally sprinkles flower petals on the bride and groom at the closing of the wedding ceremony. This is as if to say, through the extravagance of spilled flowers: May your life together be filled with comfort and ease; may it be filled with the deliciousness of flowers; may you want for nothing.

Hindu weddings in India and elsewhere also include an initial exchange of flower garlands by bride and groom, a gift of protective amulets tied to the wrists of the couple, and a recitation of family lineage. The couple is then tied together with a sash, and they walk around a ceremonial fire seven times to signify their vow to face life's challenges together. This is a beautiful symbol that you might want to incorporate in some form in your ceremony.

❧ A MARRIAGE CONTRACT ❧

The ketubah is a written marriage contract that is customarily read out loud at Jewish weddings. Developed more than a thousand years ago, it was intended to protect a woman's rights in marriage. To that end, it spelled out the financial and legal responsibilities being undertaken by the groom.

Although only the traditional wording is legal under Jewish law, many couples, both Jewish and otherwise, have chosen to write their own special versions, stating when and where they were married and detailing the promises they have made to one another. I have seen beautiful examples of such contracts, replete with elegant calligraphy and illustrations; framed and hung, they are a wonderful lasting testament to a couple's sacred vows.

CEREMONIAL FLOURISHES

Because a wedding is a gathering of friends and loved ones on behalf of the two individuals getting married, the participation of your guests is neither neutral nor irrelevant. As bride and groom, you seek their blessing, and in exchange for honoring you with the benediction of their presence, you inspire them with the example of your love. Because a wedding is really an emotional interchange of this kind, the more your guests can join in the ceremony, the more deeply felt the experience will be for everyone.

Following are a number of suggestions for special personal touches that you may want to add to your wedding. Some of them were inspired by original ceremonies at contemporary weddings; others are based on cultural customs and ancient traditions. As you will see, their general function is to involve both you and your guests more fully in the celebration. Used liberally and with imagination, they will enhance the energy, heighten the feeling, and deepen the intimacy of your wedding.

❧ CREATE A BRIDE'S PRE-WEDDING ❧ CEREMONY

If you're the bride, a short while before the wedding you might like to join with some women friends for a special ceremony. Men have bachelor parties, but aside from bridal showers, where the focus is on building a dowry, women rarely have an opportunity to bless and send off the sister who is getting married.

For example, Lydia chose to meet with her friends on the beach and asked each of them to bring a natural object (a shell, a leaf, a stone) that had meaning for her. Sitting in a circle after sharing a meal, each one of her friends spoke a blessing to Lydia that was symbolized by the object. Afterward they gathered the items into a velvet bag for her to keep.

As you depart the community of single women and join ranks with your spouse in married life, you may want to do something similar by preparing a special ritual to serve as your rite of passage. Think of exactly how you'd like this mini-ceremony to be conducted, then send invitations to your special women friends to share it with you.

When passion burns within you, remember that it was given to you for a good purpose.
—Hassidic saying

❧ BRING IN MORE LIGHT ❧

An especially lovely tradition is the lighting of the unity candle. Here both bride and groom enter, each carrying a lighted white candle. As you step up to the altar, where a single unlit candle is waiting, you use the flames of your individual candles to ignite the single large candle. This gesture symbolizes the extinguishing of individual life and the beginning of a life of union.

If you prefer a different symbolism, you may light the single large candle together, then set your individual candles, still burning, on either side of it. In this case you are symbolizing that even in marriage you retain your individuality while at the same time offering your energy to the creation of a larger union.

In the case where one or more of your parents has died, you may invite the surviving parent to light a candle to symbolize the spirit of the departed parent. This can be done when you have already taken your places just before the start of the formal ceremony, or it can be done as the usher is escorting this parent to his or her place in the congregation. Lighting a candle for the departed ones can be a lovely and very moving symbol. It ensures that in one form or another, the spirits of all of your parents are present. You may also do this if a parent is unable, for any other reason, to be present at your ceremony.

In addition, you can write a few words that either you or the officiant can pronounce to accompany a candle lighting ceremony. He or she might say, for example: "We bring the light of ourselves into the light of this union. May our unified light burn strong and bright in the future." Or, in the instance of a departed parent, the officiant or one of you may say, "In memory of the life and spirit of ____, we light this candle in our midst, in celebration of this marriage."

❧ FIND A WAY TO HONOR ❧
YOUR PARENTS

Each of you may want to choose a moment in which to make a personal tribute to your parents. For example, if the bride's father gives her away, she might turn to him before commencing the formal part of the ceremony and say, "By the way, Dad, thanks for being such a great father all these years. You were a wonderful example of a loving man, and a hard act to follow, I might add. And Mom, thanks for always taking such good care of me. I wouldn't be here without all the wonderful love you showered on me."

The point here is to give a very specific expression of appreciation that tells your parents how much you treasure and value them for all they did to bring you to this place. Include some special memories that will touch their hearts and truly acknowledge how much you value them.

You may also want to thank your spouse's parents for all they did to turn him or her into the wonderful person you're marrying:

"Thanks for bringing Joel into the world, for giving him all the love that turned him into the man who's irresistible to me. Thank you for loving him first. I promise to keep up your good work," or,

"Thanks for being such great parents. Without your love, I know she wouldn't be the wonderful person I'm marrying today."

Although all these things could be said at the reception, or even at the rehearsal dinner, finding a way to say them at the wedding, in front of all the people who are sharing the experience, will suddenly take them to a very touching depth. You'll enlarge the circle of intimacy and create a deeper bond with your parents by speaking so frankly about your feelings in the presence of your guests. These are the kinds of words parents wait a lifetime to hear; hearing them spoken at your wedding will give your parents a lifetime treasure.

✄ ALLOW YOUR PARENTS ✄ TO TALK ABOUT YOU

Invite your parents to tell a story or share a reminiscence about you. This is a wonderful way for them to go through a conscious, public ceremony of letting you go, and also of reaffirming their special relationship with you. Your father can do this just before he gives you away, or both sets of parents can do it after you've walked down the aisle or just before the address.

Along with having your parents participate, this is a lovely way of inviting your new spouse to share in some of the secrets of your childhood.

For example, the groom's father might say, "David always talked about growing up and marrying a beautiful princess. I'm so happy to see that his childhood dream is coming true."

Or it can take the form of a little inside advice. John's mother, for example, turned to his new wife, Sara, and said, "He's always late, but don't take it personally. It doesn't mean he doesn't love you." And Sara's mother told John, "She's a wonderful cook and she'll be happy to spoil you, but she'll spoil you longer—and better—if you take her out to dinner one night a week."

Once again, these words can be shared at the reception, but the mood there will be lighter. Decide if you want them shared in humor or in the sanctified spirit of the ceremony itself. In any case, they'll be all the more touching if spoken in the presence of your guests.

❧ INCLUDE A PARENTS' CEREMONY ❧ OF WELCOME

At some point in the wedding or at the reception, your parents can welcome the new member into the family. Your father may want to say for example, "Neil, it is with great joy that I welcome you into our family. I look forward to knowing you and to loving you as my new son," or, "Jan, we're so happy to have you join us as a daughter. Our hearts are open to you and we look forward to sharing our lives with you over the coming years."

Once again you can choose the spirit of this little ceremony. Do you want it to be tender, serious, and sacred? Or lighthearted, humorous, and witty? The mood you choose will probably dictate when and where you include it, but, regardless, it's a very lovely touch.

> Great loves too must be endured.
> —*Coco Chanel*

❧ SPEAK SOME PERSONAL WORDS ❧

Read a poem, the lyrics of a song, or a brief paragraph that has moved you, and, at some point during the ceremony, tell your partner how this expresses your feelings about him or her. In other words, give a minisermon of your own. Don't be afraid to make your ceremony uniquely personal by using it as an opportunity to express the deep feelings you hold in your heart for the person you are marrying.

All too often we're embarrassed by our feelings, as if the things that move us most deeply, that touch our hearts and change our lives, should be somehow shrouded in secrecy. But this is your wedding, after all, the most touching occasion of your life—so be emotionally brave. Saying some carefully chosen heartfelt words to your bride or groom, especially in front of your witnesses, will create a depth of experience you can treasure for the rest of your life.

WRITE A BEAUTIFUL WEDDING SONG

Write a special song or poem for your wedding, or rewrite the lyrics to an old favorite song ("The New Year's Eve we did the town . . . , the night we tore the goal post down . . .") For example, Fred, a musician, wrote and performed a beautiful song when he married Susie in an outdoor wedding. A total surprise, it chronicled all the special events and magical feelings of their courtship and it was a smash hit not only for Susie but for all their guests.

The real news on this planet is love—why it exists, where it came from, and where it is going. How love fares against hate and indifference is the only reliable measure of historical progress that we have.
—*Gil Bailie*

A specially tailored song can be an absolutely magical way of remembering all that is special about your relationship, putting it in a form that will be truly unforgettable. You can write (or rewrite) a song to tell the story of your romance in particular, or just to extol the virtues of love and marriage itself. Be witty, humorous, tender, or serious. Whatever your inclination, a song tailored to your experience will give an exquisitely personal touch to your wedding. If what you have in mind doesn't seem quite appropriate for the ceremony, compose it anyway, and save it for the rehearsal.

SHARE YOUR STORY

Before you say your vows, tell a wonderful little vignette or the highlights of your romance in front of the congregation. There's nothing so enchanting as a love story, and telling yours will not only delight your audience but also remind you of why you're getting married. Remembering the sweet early days of your relationship will give you a wonderful and nostalgic feeling, and will also inspire your guests. They'll be delighted to be privy to the secrets of how your love came to be. It will remind them of their own experiences of love, or inspire them to be open to the return of love in their lives. Hearing a true love story is inspirational: our spirits are all uplifted; we take heart when we're reminded that love is alive and well in the world.

❧ LET YOUR GUESTS REAFFIRM ❧ THEIR VOWS

Before or after you recite your own vows, invite the married people at your wedding to stand with their partners and reaffirm their own. You can have the officiant prepare some appropriate words, and the couples can repeat them; or the officiant can suggest that they quietly speak their own personal words of affirmation to one another.

If you decide to have the officiant lead them, you can choose a few lines from any of the vows in this book, or the officiant can lead them as follows: "I love you and thank you again for the gift of your love. Thank you for being here to love me all these years, in every way you have, in all the ways you will. I pledge again to love you for the rest of our days." Many couples attending weddings have said that hearing the vows of the bride and groom has inspired them to remember their own vows. Including this option in your ceremony is a lovely way of allowing your guests to use your wedding as the occasion to renew their own relationships.

❧ SHARE YOUR HAPPINESS ❧

Because weddings often represent great expense and personal indulgence, many couples have chosen to use their wedding as an opportunity to take note of the hardship of others and as an occasion to share their resources. Bearing this in mind, you may want to pause at a certain point in your ceremony to express thanks for your good fortune and encourage the congregation to make a contribution in your name for the homeless or to a charity of your choice.

So this doesn't come as a complete surprise to your guests, you might want to mention this in your wedding invitation. You could say, for example, "Instead of bringing us a gift, we'd ask that you make a donation to those who don't share our many blessings. We will provide a basket for this purpose at the reception. This is our way of sharing our good fortune with others and of starting out our marriage with the recognition that none of us is separate from the whole."

❧ PASS THE PEACE ❧

Before or after the convocation, you might want the officiant to suggest that everyone turn to and embrace the person closest to him or her and say a few words of greeting or blessing. You can use the traditional "Peace be with you," "And with you"; or the simpler, "I'm so glad you're here." Any greeting of this kind will more closely unite those who are celebrating your marriage with you, drawing them into a community that is truly connected in spirit and can more fully support you.

❧ INCLUDE THE CHILDREN ❧

If you have children, grown or small, you may want to invite them to say a few words—of welcome, of well-wishing, or of celebration—at your wedding ceremony: "Well, Mom, you've finally found the man of your dreams," or, "Dad, I'm really glad you found Julie. You two are wonderful together." You may also want them to serve as your attendants or to fulfill the function of "giving you away."

Whatever form it takes, do invite your children to participate in the ceremony, not only so they won't feel left out, but also because our children so often deliver the startling insights that with a lifetime of thinking we could never arrive at ourselves.

❧ DO SOMETHING OFFBEAT ❧

Suzanne and Phil had an outdoor garden wedding, and at the altar constructed a maypole with colored ribbons. Before exchanging their rings, with a beautiful recording of Renaissance music playing in the background, they wove the streamers of the maypole together, symbolizing their union, the weaving together of their two lives.

❧ CREATE A FEELING OF COMMUNITY ❧

Consider making a whole weekend of your wedding with a small group of family and friends. Rent a block of hotel rooms (Motel 6 or The Palace, depending on your budget), or a series of campsites that will allow people to share several days of the wedding experience with you.

Bringing people together for an extended period of time creates an experience of almost tribal bonding. As the community of your guests is gradually drawn together through shared time and experiences, the web of its support will be strengthened until, by the time the wedding actually occurs, you'll be surrounded by a very powerful community of support.

❧ CREATE A TALISMAN ❧

Prepare a special garment or talisman for your sweetheart to wear or carry at the wedding. Amanda, who was married in a flower-filled meadow, embroidered a shirt for her new husband, Stephen, to wear. On the inside of the collar she embroidered a heart, the words, "I love you," and the date of their wedding.

Lance prepared an exquisite "scepter of flowers" for Gwen to carry as her bridal bouquet. Rather than having something arranged by a florist, he fashioned a tower of roses laced with ribbon streamers, delivering his love and his creativity to her in this most special way.

❦ INCLUDE CREATURES GREAT ❦ AND SMALL

You may want to have your pet participate in some gracious way in your wedding ceremony. Suzette, who has three elegant whippets, had them precede her down the aisle at her outdoor garden wedding. Lucinda and Reg had a cage of white love birds ensconced in a flower-bedecked arch at the front of the church for their afternoon wedding.

❦ CHOOSE AN UNUSUAL ATTENDANT ❦

If it's appropriate, be daring and ask a man to be your bridesmaid. Elizabeth's older brother had always been her dearest, most nurturing friend, so she asked him rather than one of her girlfriends to be the attendant of honor at her wedding.

❦ INCLUDE A VOW OF SUPPORT ❦

After reciting your vows you might have the officiant address your guests and invite them to make a vow of support to you. After all, it is within the context of this community that your marriage will be enacted.

For example, the officiant might say, "Now that you have heard ＿＿ and ＿＿ recite their vows, do you, their family and friends, promise, from this day forward, to encourage them and love them, to give them your guidance, and to support them in being steadfast in the promises that they have made?" "We do."

❦ EXTEND A PERSONAL GREETING ❦

Personally greet your guests at some point early in the ceremony, before or after the formal procession. For example, after they both had arrived at the altar, Jill and Scott turned to the congregation and, walking aisle by aisle, welcomed each person individually and thanked them for coming to the wedding. When this was finished they joined hands, reestablished their position at the altar, and proceeded with the ceremony.

Particularly at a small wedding, this is a beautiful way to bring the congregation together, a chance for each person who shares the occasion to feel bonded to the bride and groom at the outset of the ceremony.

❧ BE DRAMATIC ❧

Add a fanciful, even theatrical touch to your wedding. After all, as we've said, a wedding is one of our few occasions for ceremony, take advantage of it. You have free rein to include anything you'd like, no matter how sacred or outrageous, to elevate the level of the ritual.

Jessica and Paul, who were married in Renaissance costumes on her parent's sweeping lawn, had a lutenist and a band of jugglers strolling among the guests before Jessica walked down a petal-strewn aisle. Later they introduced a baroque string quartet and four trumpets, heightening the mood in preparation for the more serious aspects of the ceremony.

What they communicated with their playful jugglers wasn't just that marriage can be a juggling act; they also reminded themselves (and their guests) that marriage is both serious and playful, fanciful and holy; rather than speaking to this truth, they had it very imaginatively dramatized.

❧ ADD MEANINGFUL RECITATIONS ❧

You may wish to have one or more persons read, almost in performance mode, a number of selections from works on love and marriage. Hearing more than one meditation on the meaning of love will be an experience of great value for your guests as well as yourselves. We all need to be reminded that love is powerful and real and that marriage is a magnificent undertaking. Hearing poetic words on the subject is one of the most deeply moving reminders we can have, so don't stint if there are many passages that move you. Invite those guests with a gift for speech to read with a beautiful voice or dramatic interpretative timing and share their gift with everyone.

❧ INCLUDE A TIME FOR SINGING ❧

At a designated point in the ceremony, perhaps at the beginning or end, invite the congregation to join you in singing a song, the words of which you have printed in advance and distributed to the guests. There's nothing like music in general, and singing in particular, to create an emotional bond—to draw people together—and there's certainly nothing more wonderful than singing a song about love.

❧ CREATE A VEIL OF BEAUTIFUL ❧ FRAGRANCE

Tell all your guests before they come to the wedding that they should bring to the ceremony a seed, herb, or spice of their choice. Shortly before the wedding, have an announcer or fair maiden invite all the guests into a room of the house or a hearth in the meadow where a pot of water has been boiling. Then have the announcer instruct each guest to drop his or her offering into the water.

As each guest does this, he or she should say a few words about the actual properties or symbolic meaning of the herbs, what they heal, create, or renew. For example: "I offer rosemary, to bring you harmony and peace"; "I bring you sage to clear away all the sorrows and the difficulties of the past." These words can be a blessing to you, and the boiling pot will emit a wonderful fragrance during and after the ceremony.

❧ HAVE A POTLUCK RECEPTION ❧

If you're on a budget (or even if you're not), consider having a potluck meal. On the invitation ask each of your friends to prepare a favorite dish (one you remember as their specialty, or one you assign to them so you're sure you'll have all the appropriate courses), and create the feast together.

You, of course, can provide all the drinks and the wedding cake, but featuring a home-made meal, the handiwork of your guests, can lend a sense of community much warmer than the usual expensive, catered affair.

❧ ENGAGE A MASTER OF CEREMONIES ❧

Choose one or several of your friends to be the master of ceremonies at your reception. Encourage this person to really put on a performance: tell funny, nostalgic, serious, or touching stories about your relationship; hopes for your future; or some spicy or even silly revelations about you and your new spouse.

Enlist your parents and friends to perform a piece of music, poem, song and dance, or just some off-the-cuff words or toasts that will delight you and your friends and add some pizzazz to the reception. Remember that along with being serious, weddings are an occasion to gather together and have a good time.

❧ ENCOURAGE SOME UNUSUAL ❧ PHOTOGRAPHY

Have one or a number of your guests circulate at the wedding and reception with disposable cameras taking candid photos of you and your guests. Your official wedding photographer can be in only one place at a time, and you'll miss lots of wonderful shots if you rely entirely on him or her. By enlisting the help of your guests, you'll capture reunions between your parents and their old friends, and your old friends with one another, to say nothing of some touching and unlikely meetings between people you've always known who haven't known one another.

One couple I know really love the photo that shows their two best friends, strangers until that day, who two years later got married to each other. Above all, by engaging some nonprofessional photographers, you'll have a joyful record of all the fun everyone had at your wedding.

Also consider videotape. Have someone who's good with the camera circulate, before, during, and after the ceremony. Some friends of mine who were virulently "anti-video" later deeply regretted not recording the moving words spoken by family and friends at their reception. And others, who had the foresight to include a video buff, were overjoyed to review the special vignettes and unforgettable words from their guests.

❧ CREATE A WEDDING MEMORY BOOK ❧

Along with photographs or a videotape of your ceremony, it's lovely to have the written words of your guests and friends. A nice way to do this is to have one of your guests or attendants make sure that every guest writes a special message—a wish, an observation about your wedding, a reflection on the special portents of the day—in a special memory book for you.

Have the person who passes the book around tell everyone that you are looking for freewheeling expression of anything your guests would like to say about the occasion, whether humorous, serious, or philosophical. Of course many guests will have already included their wishes on cards or with their gifts, but a book specifically for this purpose will provide an anthology of the wishes and wisdom of the entire group of people who shared this precious occasion with you. I especially like this idea, because it allows you to see your wedding through the eyes of all those who experienced it.

This memory book—and you'll want to choose a very pretty one—will be either situated in a conspicuous location at the reception or circulated among the guests. Instead of being the traditional guest book where people merely "sign in," the memory book will be a heartfelt collection of reflections about your wedding, a hand-written memoir that you'll love to savor in the future.

A variation on this idea is to buy a beautiful blank book and appoint one of your attendants or a special guest to be an eaves-dropping "recorder" at the ceremony and reception. It will be this person's duty to write down all the memorable things he or she over-hears as they're said by the guests at your wedding.

If you'd like to do this—and it's been truly wonderful, the several times I've seen it done—pick someone who has a flair for writing and nice sense of what's important to you. Then allow him or her to mingle like a roving reporter, writing down what's been said about you, the wedding, the ceremony, your gown, the gorgeous flowers, the wonderful sermon, or even the delectable appetizers.

Although you will have photographs or even a videotape of your wedding, it'll be especially meaningful in the future to lie in bed and turn the pages of a very special book where all the sweet, amusing, and celebratory remarks about your wedding have been hand-recorded.

❧ HAVE A POST-WEDDING CELEBRATION ❧

Many Jewish families still observe the ancient tradition of feasting for one week after the wedding to honor the bridegroom and bride. Although for most of us such extended celebrating isn't a realistic possibility, you may want to schedule a post-wedding feast, specifically commemorating your marriage, within a week, month, or six months to rekindle your love and reaffirm your vows. You may want to do this alone, with your parents, your attendants, or a few special guests. Let the wedding, and the spirit of the wedding, go on and on.

> Believe in a love that is being stored up for you like an inheritance, and have faith that in this love there is a strength and a blessing so large that you can travel as far as you wish without having to step outside it.
> —*Rilke*

WEDDING CEREMONY
worksheet

THIS WORKSHEET IS DESIGNED TO HELP YOU PLAN the particulars of your ceremony. As you see, an option for music is provided for each of the segments. Using music at all these junctures would probably result in a wedding that feels disjointed, but we have included them all so you can choose exactly where you'd like to enhance the ceremony with music.

Some people like music in the background when the words are being spoken. Others like music only in the processional and recessional portions of the wedding, with perhaps a single musical selection featured during the body of the ceremony. (If that's your choice, the best place to include it would be immediately before or after the address.) The extent to which you want to include music will depend on the kind of ceremony. All the options are provided here so you can identify precisely the points at which you want the ceremony to be emphasized by music.

Also, remember this is a worksheet, that is, a place for you to experiment with your preferences. As you list them all (and then scratch out several), you'll get a clearer sense of exactly what sort of wedding you're trying to create. The gist of it will emerge; the main emphasis will reveal itself through the various readings you choose, the vows you select, and the particular address you decide upon. As you start putting all these things together, you may find that you have to eliminate a few so the ceremony will be cohesive and not overloaded with extraneous material. Don't be afraid to eliminate as well as include; a truly beautiful wedding has focus, and moves, as we've said before, from the general to the specific.

Also, take time with the process. A wedding, just like the relationship it honors, doesn't spring up like a mushroom overnight. It will take energy, effort, and kindness to turn your vision into the unforgettable wedding of your dreams.

✤ PROCESSION ✤

....
....
....
....
....
....
....
....
....

✤ MUSICAL SELECTION(S) ✤

....
....

❧ CONVOCATION ❧

....
....
....
....
....
....
....
....
....
....

❧ MUSICAL SELECTION ❧

....
....

❧ INVOCATION ❧

....
....
....
....
....
....
....
....
....
....

❧ MUSICAL SELECTION ❧

....
....

❦ READINGS ❧

....
....
....
....
....
....
....
....
....
....

❦ MUSICAL SELECTION ❧

....
....

❦ ADDRESS ❧

....
....
....
....
....
....
....
....
....

❦ MUSICAL SELECTION ❧

....
....

❧ CONSECRATION ❧

....
....
....
....
....
....
....
....
....
....

❧ MUSICAL SELECTION ❧

....
....

❧ EXPRESSION OF INTENT ❧

....
....
....
....
....
....
....
....
....
....

❧ MUSICAL SELECTION ❧

....
....

❧ VOWS ❧

....

....

....

....

....

....

....

....

....

❧ MUSICAL SELECTION ❧

....

❧ BLESSING OF THE RINGS ❧

....

....

....

....

....

....

....

....

❧ MUSICAL SELECTION ❧

....

....

❧ EXCHANGING OF THE RINGS ❧

....

....

....

....

....

....

....

....

....

❧ MUSICAL SELECTION ❧

....

....

❧ PRONOUNCEMENT OF MARRIAGE ❧

....

....

....

....

....

....

....

....

❧ MUSICAL SELECTION ❧

....

....

❧ BENEDICTION ❧

....
....
....
....
....
....
....
....

❧ MUSICAL SELECTION ❧

....
....

❧ RECESSION ❧

....
....
....
....
....
....
....
....

❧ MUSICAL SELECTION ❧

....
....